To

Mum,

on Mothers Day

Love

from

Carol & Adrian

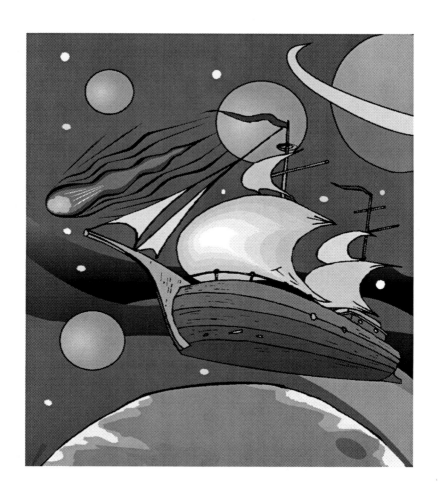

2001: A POETRY ODYSSEY STOKE

Edited by Carl Golder

First published in Great Britain in 2001 by
YOUNG WRITERS
Remus House,
Coltsfoot Drive,
Peterborough, PE2 9JX
Telephone (01733) 890066

HB ISBN 0 75432 930 5
SB ISBN 0 75432 931 3

FOREWORD

Young Writers was established in 1991 with the aim to promote creative writing in children, to make reading and writing poetry fun.

This year the 2001: A Poetry Odyssey competition again proved to be a tremendous success with over 50,000 entries received nationwide.

The amount of hard work and effort put into each entry impressed us all, and is reflective of the teaching skills in schools today.

The task of selecting poems for publication was a difficult one but nevertheless, an enjoyable experience. We hope you are as pleased with the final selection in *2001: A Poetry Odyssey Stoke* as we are.

CONTENTS

Endon High School

Andrew Chell	49
David Arthur Ruddle	49
Sarah Twyford	50
Katie Adams	50
Sam Dawson	51
Grace Barrett	52
Victoria Rhodes	52
James Thomas	53
Matthew Smith	54
Louise Pezzaioli	54
Katie Mayer	55
Emma Bentley	56
Darren Parker	57
Elizabeth Williams	58
Katie Belfield	59
Adam Williamson	60
Faye Bibbey	61
Andrew Bradshaw	61
Rebecca Kelly	62
Louise Adele Butler	62
Nicholas Errington	63

Haywood High School

Daniel Downing	64

Kemball School

Martyn Lymer, David Gallimore & Daniel Hope	65

Painsley Catholic High School

Marianne King	65
Martin Bland	66
Holly Cheadle	66
John Mills	67
Dominic Bridgwood	68

Ben Cornwall	99
Francesca Brown	99
Claire Richards	100
Jack Woolley	100
Lucy Malcolm	101
Avril Taylor	101
Joanna Handy	102
Steve Long	103
Samantha Davey	104
Suzannah Cordon	105
Lauren Tilstone	106
Laura Parry	107
Lucy Woolliscroft	108
Nicola Collier	109
Esther Porter	110
Laura Rigby	110
Sarah Wilks	111
Laura Campbell	111
Katie Withington	112
Cora Moodie	112
Katie Stanier	113
Matthew Hurst	113
Darren Grzesiak	114
Charlotte Randall	114
Jennifer Keeling	115
Francesca Talbot	115
Siobhan McAulay	116
Clare Beech	116
Joanne Parry	117
Anthony Callan	117
Steven Luke	118
Simon Weston	119
Rachel Nixon	120
Tawny Hill	120
Simon Carnwell	121
Lauretta Fernando-Smith	121

The Poems

ANIMALS

A is for antelope, running free,
B is for bear, fishing for tea,
C is for cheetah, running so fast,
D is for Dalmatian, he's found a bone at last!
E is for elephant, living on the plain,
F is for frog, he's jumping again,
G is for Great Dane, a very big dog,
H is for hen, who sits on a log,
I is for ibex, a very strange bird,
J is for jaguar, whose roar can be heard,
K is for kangaroo, who leaps and bounces,
L is for lion, who roars and pounces,
M is for mouse, who's really so small,
N is for narwhal, who's got a mysterious call,
O is for otter, who leaps and swims,
P is for penguin, who has black and white wings,
Q is for quagga, who's a cross between a zebra and a horse,
R is for rabbit, he's got a fluffy tail, of course!
S is for seal, who plays by the sea,
T is for tiger, who hunts for his tea,
U is for umbrella bird, who has a beautiful wing,
V is for viper, who doesn't dare sing,
W is for walrus, who lives in the sea,
X is for x as in fox, as sly as can be,
Y is for yak, which isn't a horse,
Z is for zebra, that's the end of course!

Wendy Harvey (13)
Abbey Hill School

PEOPLE

A is for Aaron, who eats cake all day,
B is for Ben, who plays in the hay,
C is for Christine, whose laugh's like a bark,
D is for Daniel, who plays in the dark,
E is for Edward, who plays with his finger,
F is for Freddie, whose teddy is called Binger,
G is for Gregory, who sucks his thumb all day,
H is for Harry, who swims in the bay,
I is for Ivory, who plays in the bin,
J is for Jack, who sits on a pin,
K is for Kim, who licks a lollipop all day,
L is for Leonard, who works for no pay,
M is for Mum, whose best friend is May,
N is for Norman, who kisses May Young,
O is for Owen, whose song is sung,
P is for Paul, who is good at climbing a wall,
Q is for Quin, who gives money to the poor,
R is for Richard, who rocks on his chair,
S is for Sarah, who has shiny hair,
T is for Tom, who blows kisses all day,
U is for Uwen, who is good at the bay,
V is for Vince McManus, whose mate dances,
W is for Willy, who likes to run all day,
X is for Xedy, who is good at making buns,
Y is for Yunis, who likes to wish,
Z is for Zoe, who likes to fish.

Ashley Callaghan (12)
Abbey Hill School

NAMES

A is for Arthur, who is a sweetie,
B is for Ben, who likes Betty,
C is for Carl, who plays with a box,
D is for Dwayne, who has a fox,
E is for Edward, who plays on the swings all day,
F is for Freddie, who swims in the bay,
G is for Georgina, who is silly,
H is for Harry, who has a friend called Billy,
I is for Ian, who eats a lolly with a lick,
J is for Jo, who hits with her stick,
K is for Kelly, who looks at leaves,
L is for Lucy with goofy teeth,
M is for Mark, who bites his pencil,
N is for Nathan, who draws with a stencil,
O is for Owen, who plays with a ball,
P is for Peter, who plays in the hall,
Q is for Quentin, who plays with a bear,
R is for Ray, who rocks on his chair,
S is for Sarah, who sees a bay,
T is for Tommy, who eats hay,
U is for Uma, who is a pain,
V is for Vincent, who plays out in the rain,
W is for Wayne, who eats his jumper,
X is for Xavier, who kicks a bumper,
Y is for Yunis, who thinks he is hot and
Z is for Zoe, who sleeps in a cot.

Josephine Pond 12)
Abbey Hill School

MY DOG TOBY

My dog Toby is my friend
He is very nice,
Sometimes he drives me round the bend
And prefers chasing cats to mice.

Toby is brown and white
He has floppy ears,
I have to say he does not bite
I have lived with him for two years.

Toby is sometimes daft
Say 'Walkies' and his tail wags,
When he got in bed I laughed
And sometimes he breaks his tags.

I love Toby and he loves me
He is very cute,
Without him I don't know where I'd be
I'll never give him the boot.

Nigel Rigby (11)
Abbey Hill School

DOLPHINS

My dream is to swim with dolphins,
In the deep blue sea.
As the sun shines on them,
They dance wild and free.

They love to be with humans,
And never seem to mind,
Just stroke them and touch them,
They certainly have the time.

They jump so long,
In the seas high tide,
For miles and miles,
Almost touching the sky.

One day I'll meet them,
Just you wait and see,
I'll be happy and excited,
Yes, this is the life for me.

Ceris Everson (12)
Birches Head High School

THE HOMELESS MAN

I saw him in the street, alone he sat,
Dressed in rags, upon a mat.
He looked so sad, as he sighed,
Seeing him made me bleary-eyed.
People walked by, they don't really care,
The poor old man sits, in great despair.
They don't want to look, they don't want to know,
Hoping next day he'll walk off and go.
There he sits in the same old place,
There's pain in his eyes, on that dirty face.
As weeks go by, I still think of him,
When it goes cold, or at night when it's dim.
He's still sitting, hoping that help will appear
But optimism weakens, as winter draws near.
I went out one day, in the cold air,
But to my horror, the man wasn't there.

Amy Smith (15)
Birches Head High School

SONNET - MY NAN

Although you have gone you feel so near!
Oh how I wish I could have said goodbye,
But now it's too late, that's what I fear.
I know that you wouldn't want me to cry,
I keep all our memories in my heart.
I hope you're happy wherever you are,
We had a special bond right from the start!
I look to the sky and wish on a star,
That I might see you again some day soon.
Are you in Heaven looking down on me?
You shone so bright like at night so does the moon!
Should I wait, be patient, is that the key?
It seems so cruel that God took you away,
Without you Nan we remain in dismay!

Lisa Glass (13)
Birches Head High School

BONFIRE NIGHT

Bonfire lit with Guy Fawkes on top,
Fireworks going off left, right and centre,
Beautiful colours everywhere,
Amazing sparklers in every kid's hand,
Fireworks waking up little babies,
Shining lights in the sky,
The man at the barbecue is handing out hot dogs,
I love Bonfire Night,
It's so great,
I wish it was bonfire night every night of the year.

Ashley Mochan (12)
Birches Head High School

HALLOWE'EN

It's All Hallows Eve and the ghosts are out,
fearful victims scream and shout.

The creatures of the night awaken once more,
what does this special night have in store?

All people are asleep while the spirits ring out the bells
the witching hour comes as the clock strikes twelve.

Brain of zombie, and eye of newt,
blood sucked by a vampire in a red and black suit.

Pumpkins filled with light gleam,
but their faces are so sinister, they look so mean.

It's All Hallows Eve and the ghosts are out,
'Trick or Treat' is what they shout.

Sandra Wagg (13)
Birches Head High School

THE MONSTER POEM

Its eyes are as wide as a back end of a wide load lorry,
Its skin is like bubbles in a big bubble bath,
Its legs are as thin as a twig on a big tree.

Its claws are as long as a trunk of an elephant,
Its breath smells like the backs of Easy Street,
Its arms are as hairy as a big spider that crawls up his back.

Its tongue is as long as a slimy snake,
Its ears are as small as a tiny little mouse that hunts for food,
Its mouth is as long as an old person's walking stick.

Zoe-Ann Derricott (13)
Birches Head High School

THE SILVERSTONE EXPERIENCE

It was the most thrilling feature of my life,
On the 16th of September,
Viewing something memorable,
To treasure and remember.

When I arrived at my destination,
My eyes ablaze with joy,
Ford, Vauxhall, Nissan and Honda,
I pondered, I am a fortunate boy.

I disembarked from the car,
Delighted by this place,
I sprinted to the Brookland's suite,
At such an immense pace.

I searched on the index for Total Fina Elf
I discovered it with exceptional vision,
So that was to be my hospitality,
And I found it with remarkable precision.

So the racing commenced on the Silverstone circuit,
Its duration was all day,
Then came the superlative feature race,
Which began without delay.

The tremendous tours were distant,
To the B-class contestants at the rear,
Their brake pads ignited with an illuminous effulgence,
And their windscreens glistening and clear.

The race ended in emphatic style,
With Honda victorious in the end,
But the championship had been decided,
On the final bend.

David Cegielski (13)
Birches Head High School

THE BOY IN THE CORNER

Why do people get picked on
If they're slightly different,
If they are tall or wear glasses,
Just like the boy in the corner.

Why do people call others names
And push and shove them?
If they bump into them by accident?
Just like the boy in the corner.

Why do people take your money
And leave you with no lunch,
Then you get hungry,
Just like the boy in the corner.

Why do people take your homework,
And stamp on it in the mud,
Then you get into trouble,
Just like the boy in the corner,

Why do people hit each other,
And kick and punch them,
Until they're screaming in pain,
Just like the boy in the corner.

Then they think their life's a mess,
And it can't get any better,
So they go and kill themselves
Just like the boy in the corner.

Now there's another boy in the corner
Standing all alone.

Joanne Amison (12)
Birches Head High School

LAZING IN PARADISE

My heaven, my rapture, my ecstasy;
A gleeful, euphoric, vast paradise.
I wander, the sand, it blows around me,
No despair and no regret of the price.
My despondencies, my decline, my gloom;
All fade away when I am at the beach.
I fret, why must it be over so soon?
Far from my woe; I do not want to preach,
The sea for rapport, nobody to blight.
I hear the waves, the sea and I am one.
I gaze at the sands, such a tranquil sight.
The burden of urban chaos is gone.
I'll spend my life here, lazing in the sun,
I might be snoozing but the sun shines on.

Jamie Rathbone (13)
Birches Head High School

A TYPICAL SCHOOL DAY

My head is buried deep in my hands,
I can hear people discussing their weekend plans,
I just sit and watch them, they're having fun,
I wish I could join in with someone - anyone,
I feel I'm in a large black hole,
Somewhere round about,
No one ever hears what I say,
Even when I shout!

I stand up and look around,
My eyes just seem to focus on the ground,
I'm not able to hear any sounds,
Other than the muffled voices of others and
The thoughts whizzing around in my head,
Why can't everyone just be kind to each other?

I often wonder what people would say
If I joined them - to go and play,
I really do try my best
To fit in with everyone,
Why can't I be like all the rest,
And just have a bit of fun?

Beverly Turner (13)
Birches Head High School

THE SEA AND SAND

Sitting on the warm golden sand,
Letting some trickle through my hand,
Watching the waves crashing on the beach,
Exploding from a place so far to reach.
The blue summer's sky,
So far away and high,
With not a cloud in sight,
Will be so very cold at night.
A feeling of joy creeps into my mind,
And even through I try, I can't seem to find
The sadness I have felt so long.
I believe I have been very wrong,
About this beautiful and peaceful place.
So now I let myself face
The blue sea, far out, calling,
To the gentle wind that is calmly falling,
And rustling my tangled brown hair.
The world now seems to be so fair,
And I wish I could sit here forever,
Gazing at the gorgeous beach that never
Fails to piece up a ruined life, or join up a broken heart.

Javairia Latif (13)
Birches Head High School

FARAWAY PLACE

The journey to the faraway place
So comfy that I cannot say.
Travelling miles up in the sky,
with the clouds that float by.

Looking through the window, see another plane,
Smoke coming out like an old steam train.
It starts to fade as the plane goes further,
Into the clouds like a sliver of silver.

Asked to see the pilot,
They say his name is Jim.
Can't wait to see the cockpit,
I'm going in a min.

Walking down the aisle,
Which doesn't seem far.
Knock on the door, walk inside,
Wow what a view from this other side.

Back in my seat, they say we are nearly there,
They give us a parachute and say a little prayer.
I look at the hostess, she is laughing with glee,
She says that the joke was on me.

Take a deep breath, swallow really hard,
Wheels on the ground stay in your seat until we turn around.
Off the plane now, the sun is really hot,
It has been a long journey, but well worth the lot.

Michelle Booth (16)
Birches Head High School

FRIENDS IN THE NIGHT

The moon shines brightly in the sky
Her secrets safe on the dark side
What is she hiding, we might never know
On that dark side that she will never show.

I wonder if she is sad
So far away and all alone
The many friends she has never had
The happiness she had never known.

She bears so many craters and scars
Unlike all of the other stars
Shooting stars and meteors pass her by
While flying through the twinkling sky.

They never wave or say hello
Their minds are riddled with ignorance
Until one day a gentleman
He turned around and just by chance,

He said goodnight my fellow moon
And hopefully I'll see you soon
And from then almost every night
He blew her a kiss and flew on by.

The moon was happy; she had a friend
This story simply just had to have a happy end.

Elizabeth Tute (13)
Birches Head High School

WHAT IS PINK?

What is gold? A jewel is gold
Sparkling and shining so bold.

What is grey? A hippopotamus is grey
Sludgy, muddy and rolls in hay.

What is red? A jumper is red
A sign of Birches Head.

What is purple? A tie is purple
Like a fresh baked blueberry pie.

What is blue? The sky is blue
On its clearest day.

What is black? A cloud is black
With rain gathering inside.

What is silver? The moonlight is silver
Shining so bright.

What is pink? A child's cheeks are pink
A sign of laughter and joy.

Danielle Fox (13)
Birches Head High School

WILL LIFE GO ON?

In one hundred years time what will life be like?
Will the hours be worshipped? Will Big Ben strike?
Will all countries join? Will we have a woman president?
Will my house be a hotel for any resident?

In two hundred years time what will life be like?
Will the planets rotate? Will the stars twinkle at night?
Will snow and rain still fall sometimes?
Will the hot, blistering sun still brightly shine?

In the next millennium what will life be like?
Will people be aliens? Will animals have life?
Will extinction kill everything here today?
Or will everything be forever this way?

Adele Hodgen (13)
Birches Head High School

MURDER

I hear a scream
Everything around goes dark
I hear a moan.

I panic and run,
Was he dead? Could he be saved?
Where do I run?

I run to the lane
And jump into my sports car
And race down the road.

The chase is on
Is he behind me or not?
What have I just done?

Should I call the cops
Or should I go back and check
If he's still alive.

I called the police
And they made a search for him
They said they would phone.

Colin Everson (13)
Birches Head High School

EXAMS

Exams are so boring they make you think
After you have finished you can relax
But when they are done you have to re-think
And accelerate your brain to the max.

You need a pen or pencil to write with
Maybe a ruler for drawing a line
You will need to write to keep you alive
All desks graphited on that lovely pine.

The teachers walk up and down the long aisle
Step by step they go checking your work
Leaving footprints on the beautiful aisles
So you can stop acting like a big berk.

Seconds, minutes and hours all feel the same
This is how you get to the hall of fame.

Chris Willshaw (13)
Birches Head High School

THE HIGHLANDER

The storm clouds rolled across the scarred landscape,
As a man walked towards a mountain on the edge of the landscape.
He had seen the battle that had scarred his homeland and
Had seen many more homes destroyed within his everlasting life.
He reached the mountain and stared towards the sky,
He now knew where mankind had gone after desolating
Their home world.
Nothing lived on what they called Earth,
It was completely empty, scarred by a millennia of wars.
He stared towards the sky and vanished leaving
But only the clouds to move on this deceased world.

Neil McCue (15)
Birches Head High School

When I Am Outside

The sky is nice and blue
I see it every day
Sometimes it is cloudy
Or maybe even rainy.

I see some seagulls every day
Flying in the sky
I wonder if it lives here
Or maybe passing by.

When I go out to play
The weather must be nice
But when it is raining
I sometimes stay inside.

James Davies (12)
Birches Head High School

Sea And Sky

As I'm sailing across the
Deep blue sea,
I look up towards the
Cloudless sky,
Where I see the sun is setting,
And the moon is rising high.

The waves of the sea are rolling past,
Slowly bobbing me up and down,
As the sun disappears over the horizon,
I stare at the stars in the sky.

Rebecca Foster (13)
Cheadle High School

THE COUNTRYSIDE

In the fresh country meadows
Where the grass grows green,
Here are just a sample
Of the things I've seen.

Birds in the treetops,
Fishes in the stream,
It looks so unreal,
Just like a dream.

Flowers in the fields,
Rabbits in the grass,
And the warm, golden sunshine,
Shiny as brass.

Berries in the hedgerow,
Fruits on the tree,
It's a beautiful sight
For all to see.

In the fresh country meadows
Where the grass grows green,
Here are just a sample
Of the things I've seen.

Nicola Ward (12)
Cheadle High School

WANTED

Has anyone got
A puppy to spare,
A cat or a rabbit,
Or even a hare?

I'd cherish a pony,
I'd care for a horse,
If I'm offered a camel
I'd love it of course.

I'd take in a hamster,
I'd quite like a rat,
A toad would be welcome
Or even a bat.

A beetle that's friendly
Would find that I'm kind.
Snake, lizard or earthworm
I'm sure I don't mind.

I don't mind how big,
I don't mind how small,
I just want a pet
That can walk, fly or crawl.

Richard Buxton (11)
Cheadle High School

FIREWORKS

The bonfire's all prepared,
It's all surrounded by wire,
And people watch in amazement
As Guy Fawkes is thrown on the fire.

The adults prepare the fireworks,
Such as sparklers, Catherine wheels and rockets.
The children prepare to be amazed,
And cold hands go into pockets.

The jumping jacks are jumping,
And hopping all around.
There aren't any colours at all,
And they bang when they leave the ground.

The rockets go up in the air,
And shine a ray of light.
The rockets explodes into a Union Jack,
Made of colours, red, blue and white.

The rockets go off with a bang,
Then explodes and lights up the air.
Then all of a sudden more go off,
It's beautiful everywhere.

The children feel spots on their noses,
It's now beginning to rain.
The fire dies down as before,
And shreds of Guy remain.

Jennifer Stubbs (11)
Cheadle High School

EXTRAORDINARY WEATHER

A clap of thunder,
A flash of light,
Thunder and lightning strikes,
It's all in the sky tonight.

Drip, drop, drip
Went the rain,
Drip, drop, drip
On my windowpane.

The sun is coming out,
He's shining just for me,
He's shining down the streets,
He's shining out with glee.

Woo, woo,
The wind is getting stronger,
People shout 'Tornado!'
And hide away for longer.

Snow is falling down,
Children shout 'Snow!'
Parents moan and groan
While others shout 'Oh no!'

The pond is all iced over,
The fish can hardly see,
We're going to chip away the ice,
And set the fishes free.

Kayleigh Johnson (12)
Cheadle High School

Manchester United Vs Manchester City

Hi! I'm Alex and I live in Stafford,
And my favourite ground is the big one Old Trafford,
My dad got tickets to see Man United,
He asked me to come I was very excited.

We got there, my seat was number 232,
And after two minutes I needed the loo,
I got back to my seat and oh what a pity,
The first goal was scored by Manchester City.

Right after centre we got a goal back,
It was scored by Cole and boy he was fast,
Beckham raced up the wing,
You could hear the crowd sing.

He crossed it to Nicky Butt
Who flicked it with his foot,
It came through to Cole
Who scored a great goal.

Everyone knew Dwight Yorke was a threat,
Seven times this season he had stuck it in the net,
He crashed to the floor, the defenders said 'What!'
As the referee pointed to the penalty spot.

Irwin stepped up to take the penalty kick,
Anyone could have taken it, just take your pick,
He blasted it home to make the score two,
One minute later the final whistle blew.

Two-one was the score, what a brilliant game,
I wish they'd score more but I'm still glad I came,
Now it's back to the car for my dad and me,
It's not the end of my treat, it's McDonald's for tea.

Alex Smith (12)
Cheadle High School

EXTRAORDINARY WEATHER

E very second my heart beats, lightning comes down from the dull, dark sky

X- raying the town I live in to see what it can hit down next.

T errifying trouble! The clouds have got written on them,

R oaring through the night, the thunder will last I know.

A ngrier and angrier the storm is getting worse and worse by every second,

O ccasionally the wind would come like a pack of wolves.

R un away from this dangerous, leashing storm,

D are you? I think of all the terrors it will bring . . . *death!*

I wonder when this will stop, it may stop suddenly or not at all

N ever in my life has it gone this bad.

A lready it has just past midnight and this storm should be calming down

R acing against the wind like a greyhound, the lightning was winning a race,

Y et in the distance it looks like the back end of the storm.

W ill this ever stop I ponder . . . Will it?

E nraged this storm is getting worse,

A ll you can hear is crackles of thunder and screams of fright.

T he tension builds and increases.

H ear the rain, how it bangs on the windows like loud drums being played.

E ventually the storm . . . stops!

R ain goes, thunder and lightning goes, everything is so peaceful And still,

        Until . . .

Sarah Butcher (13)
Cheadle High School

MY DOG

My dog is a gymnast as fine as fine can be,
He also does crosswords and watches BBC.
You should see him doing cartwheels, he even taught me.

He was in the dog Olympics, he's won Crufts fifty times,
By the age of two weeks he was composing nursery rhymes.
He jumps over hurdles at fifty miles an hour,
If you look carefully, he's got a superpower.

My dog is a gymnast, he performs superbly,
He also does javelin and watches BBC.
You should see him doing handstands, he even taught me.

He's starred in twenty operas, he was in Titanic too,
Oh yes, please believe me it's definitely true.
He is a Grand Master he's been in Wimbledon twice,
He invented an invention which exterminates mice.

My dog is an athlete as superb as can be,
He also does dancing and watches TV.
You should see him doing the pole vault, he even taught me.

He's got the body of a wrestler, he also kicks down doors,
Be careful next-door neighbours, he could kick down yours.
He drives a Mercedes, refuses to wear any leads,
He sits cross-legged on the floor and just reads.

My dog is an acrobat, he isn't nothing cheap,
But right now at this time he's on the floor *asleep!*

Jo Bradbury (12)
Cheadle High School

It's Not Fair!

We've heard it said in so many ways,
At home, at school, that little phrase,
But do any of us know just what it means?
Why should we use it like we do now
With no reason as to why or how?
It has no meaning to us it seems.
When something doesn't go the way
We think it should from day to day,
Is it fair for you or me?
Not everything is fair in life,
Hunger, illness, death and strife,
Things have a reason, can't you see?
Is it fair that people like us
Have the freedom of our own choice
While others have to go without?
Should we go along with it
Just because it seems to fit?
Is that what this is all about?
Why is it that we have the freedom
And are never put in prison
For thinking freely and speaking our mind?
Are we superior to other countries
Just because of our nationalities?
Is this the way of all mankind?
The world is but a tangled web;
It's not fair is all that's said,
We hardly ever mean it - so why say it?

Heather Wheat (13)
Cheadle High School

ROLLER-COASTER

Up and down and up and down,
Up the hill and down the slope.
Up and up and up and up then,
Doooown we go.

Round and round and round we go,
Spinning round and going down.
Going up, then spinning round,
Down and down whilst going round.

Everyone screaming
As loud as they can.
Some glad to get off,
Some wanting to go on again and again.

Some people like roller-coasters,
Some people don't.
Maybe you like them,
Maybe you don't?

They're normally very scary,
And for some people they're fun.
I find them very exciting,
Do you love or do you loathe them?

Geri Histead (13)
Cheadle High School

A BREATHTAKER

A rumble, a gasp,
Lightning lit up the sky,
A clap of thunder,
A frightful cry.

The windows rattled,
They wouldn't hold,
We were evacuated
Out into the cold.

The sea was wild,
So were the people,
The church was gliding,
So was the steeple.

Down into the shelter
We stayed for hours,
We came up,
Trembled and cowered.

It was breathtaking,
The hotel was gone,
And where there were clouds
Now was the sun.

Amy Howourth (12)
Cheadle High School

THE MONSTER AWAKES

The monster lying on the bed,
Dusty and rusty
And wrapped up in bandages.

To bring him back to life
Was a great risk,
But one Aunt Frankenstein was
Willing to take.

Aunt Frankenstein pressed go,
The engines started whirring,
The thundering and lightning stirring,
Frans released the kites,
Igor raised the table.

The needles reached halfway,
And raised up in to the red zone,
And all of a sudden,
The needles reached *'danger'*,
And then sunk right back down again.

'Bring the bed down' Igor shouted.
So the monster, lying so still on the bed
Suddenly raised his head.
He took his first breath.
He's finally awake exclaimed Aunt Frankenstein.

Sarah Lawton (13)
Cheadle High School

THEATRE

I know my lines,
I know my songs,
I know my moves,
How can I go wrong?

Make-up on,
Props are ready,
Audience in,
I'm playing Eddie.

Lights go down,
Mikes switched on,
Silence falls,
Help! I'm on.

The first song fades,
The music dies,
I'm on, I'm on,
Quick let me hide.

The last song fades,
The curtain falls,
The audience cheers,
The curtain calls.

Will I ever act on a west end stage?
Will I ever reach the dizzy heights?
Will I ever see my name in lights?
Is this a dream?

Helen Ewen (12)
Cheadle High School

SISTERS

Sisters are always messing with phones,
I wonder why they're always bone (idle).
Messing with make-up, chatting up boys,
They're always messing with my toys.
Shut up, shut up their mums cry,
Don't you mess with my hair dye.
The trouble with big sisters are they're older than me,
And always reminding us so frequently.
They are always spending their mum's money,
Never helping to clean out the bunny.
Booming music comes from upstairs,
When I walk past they always glare.
Stay out of my room they say to me,
But I'm only asking you to come for tea.
Oh yeah, came the answer flying at me,
I love my sister as you can see!

Samantha Bryan (11)
Cheadle High School

MY CAT

My cat is black,
He sits on my fireplace mat,
He waits for me to come home from school
While he drinks his water cool,
When he sleeps you'd think he'd curl
But not my cat he's like a big girl,
All stretched out over my bed,
Then he starts jumping around my head,
Scratching and purring and hurting my leg
But I still love him even if he shares my bed.

Ashton Twigge (11)
Cheadle High School

JOEY MY COUSIN

Joey's three, nearly four,
The cutest you ever saw.
This little angel,
My little friend
But he can drive you round the bend.
Sweet as sugar, cuddly and cute
Even in his birthday suit.
He loves to watch a friend called TV,
Everyone says he gets it from me.
Light blond hair, big blue eyes,
He likes chips but not healthy pies.
This little devil runs around
Making a screeching, horrid sound.
He'll sit down nearby and start to yell
Right after he's told you 'I'm not very well.'
Then he goes to bed as quiet as a mouse,
After he's trashed the whole of the house.

Rebecca Stubbs (11)
Cheadle High School

SUMMER DAYS

I sit here on my bed
Trying to think in my head,
Is there such a day
When the grass is about to be turned to hay,
And I lie in the grassland,
Wondering why does the sun look like sand
As the gentle breeze blows a scent so strong,
It takes me into a hazy song!

Sarah Spooner (12)
Cheadle High School

MOVING HOUSE

Moving house to a different place
Has to be done at a very fast pace.
Tables, chairs, cabinets too,
I have lots of things I need to do.
Unloading your stuff into the new house,
All that walking you have legs like a mouse.
Carrying, walking, moving around all the time,
Can't wait for that lager and lime.
Your first night's gone, get up early in the morning,
Getting ready for the big house warming.
After all that time, the year's gone by,
We start a new beginning, a new bright sky.

Jonathan Shenton (11)
Cheadle High School

HOMELESS

He steps in a corner,
He sleeps in an alley,
He goes for days on an empty belly,
He's homeless,
He hasn't got a car, no place to sleep,
He hasn't had food for at least a week,
Why is he homeless? Why, why?
He's got no money to buy, buy, buy!
We think he's dirty, we think he's small,
In fact I know him very, very well.
He scrounges like the seagulls on the seashore,
He sits on a corner asking for more.

Lee Grantham (13)
Cheadle High School

AUTUMN

When autumn begins the leaves change colour,
Some get lighter, others get duller,
The leaves then fall off the trees,
Children like to kick them as they please.

Horse chestnut trees grow a seed
Which are spiky and sometimes make you bleed.
The seed is called a conker.
Children like to pick the spiky seeds.

Some flowers shrivel up on their stem,
People pick their bulbs or seeds to save them.
The bulbs or seeds are kept till spring,
They are then planted to begin a new living.

Leane Hassall (11)
Cheadle High School

GOAL

The ball hit the net with a dazzling stroll,
With a shout from the crowd which was really loud!
Minutes and minutes quickly went by,
The other team went in with a sigh.
Half-time came to have a break,
The manager said 'Hurry have a cake!'
They went back on, ninety minutes came,
They ran away, proud of the game.
Only one goal,
But the ball hit the net with a dazzling stroll.

Craig Wood (12)
Cheadle High School

VOLCANO!

There's a volcano which erupted yesterday,
Winding itself round, round all the way down.

Fluorescent orange lava flowing through the streets,
Leaving buildings crashing down in a big dusty heap.

People are screaming, shouting, running, knowing that
Their lives are at risk.

Then everything is silent . . .

As you gaze at the frightening mess,
What had happened you easily guess,

As you look everything is crisp like crumble and crinkle.

Everywhere is black like a witch's black cat,
Covered in dust, everything is lost,
We must leave this horrible sight,
Start again with a new leaf, with a new life.

Charlotte Buffey (11)
Cheadle High School

THE WORLD

Japan, Taiwan, I've been to them all,
Even the Eiffel Tower that's tall.
Underground, overground,
I've been to them all.
I love countries, I love them all,
Places abroad or places local,
Aeroplanes and other transport, they get you there.
I love countries, I love them all,
I love the world and its places.

Beth Coleman (11)
Cheadle High School

MY PERFECT FAMILY

My mum can be a pain,
Sometimes she drives me insane.
She's always telling me off,
I only have to cough.

My dad is always sleeping,
It would make no difference if a horn was beeping.
The only time he wakes up is to eat,
Then he spends the rest of his time in his seat.

My brothers are always running about,
When you tell them off they just run, scream and shout.
The house is always a wreck,
Sometimes you just want to strangle them around the neck.

Despite all these things I have said,
There is nowhere I'd rather be than in my own bed.
We can all laugh about the good times and bad
Which makes us the most perfect family this world has ever had.

Leanne Colclough (12)
Cheadle High School

MY CAT

My cat is black and white,
She likes to stay in my room all night.
Sometimes upon my pillow she lies,
And purrs at me through half-closed eyes.
As soon as daylight appears,
She starts to lick at my ears.
'Wake up' she cries, 'I want some dinner!'

Naomi Redman (11)
Cheadle High School

EXTRAORDINARY WEATHER

I'm sitting in my room,
And it's getting rather late,
Lightning divides the sky
Like a crack in a plate.

Storm clouds, storm clouds,
Dark, damp and drab,
Some look fab,
And some look like a crab.

Thumping thunder, whooshing wind,
Doors slamming, windows rattling
Just like an unreal battle.

Brisk and bracing cold night air,
Swirly sky and stirring storm,
A spine-chilling chill,
Oh why can't it just be tranquil.

Laura-Jane Bevans (12)
Cheadle High School

EXTRAORDINARY WEATHER

It's the hottest day ever,
Will it ever cool down?
I hope it does
Because everyone's face is a frown.

It's the coldest day ever,
Will it ever warm up?
My hands are so numb
I can't even hold a cup.

It's the windiest day ever,
Will it ever stop blowing?
I hope it does
Because I want to go rowing.

It's the calmest day ever,
I like the weather like this.
It's not too hot, cold or windy,
It's just bliss.

Helen Lomax (12)
Cheadle High School

WISHING

Why wish the hours and days away,
Some do say.
I wish I had the time to come,
Which had passed away.
Things I'd do and things I'd not,
Why do we say, this foolish lot?

What has come and what's been done,
'Tis part of the battle, the journey's run.

To wish this way,
Would not erase the fateful day,
Which weaves around us,
Wher'er we may.

One day won,
Is one day done,
And is part of the journey,
Our life has to run.

Amy Northwood (12)
Cheadle High School

SUMMER

I love this time of the year!

Sitting in the warmth of the sun's rays,
Just lying there, deep in thought while the waves crash in against
the killer rocks.
Go into the sea and see all those beautifully dazzling fish weaving
along the seabed,
The sand, so annoying! Easing its way into every crack and corner
in sight.

Look at all the colours around you,
The calm blue of the drifting ocean,
The sparkling yellow of the sun's deep rays reflecting off the sea,
The pleasant green of those gently flapping palm leaves in the
tranquil breeze.

I love this time of year - *summer.*

Elizabeth Spooner (13)
Cheadle High School

CHRISTMAS DAY

Hip, hip hooray it's Christmas Day,
Sacks hanging on the chimney tall,
I wonder if it will snow today,
If it does then how deep will it fall?

There's presents waiting to be unwrapped,
Nan sitting in the corner with a cat on her lap,
Mother in the kitchen cooking dinner for all,
Father trying to get the lights working in the hall.

Sister's upstairs getting their make-up on,
I'm downstairs having lots of fun,
Grandad in the garden letting the dog have a run,
And we are all waiting for Aunty to come.

Christmas dinner is all finished and done,
Dad's sleeping with his trousers undone,
Mum's watching telly with a silly hat on,
Nan in the kitchen getting the washing-up done.

Karl Sharp (11)
Cheadle High School

IT

Along the grass it crept, it crawled
Even though it's young and bald,
The shape of it is big and round,
Its tummy wobbles on the ground.

As I watched this creature move,
Its head sort of wiggled in a groove,
This thing in its mouth which it kept sucking,
Its back legs which kept bucking.

It almost hit me the silly creature,
One thing that stood out was this peculiar feature
In its mouth, it had two teeth,
A big fat tongue that lies beneath.

The creature which I've been talking about
Is only my baby sister, there's no need to shout!

Talia Sales (11)
Cheadle High School

SUMMER

Butterflies are fluttering here and there,
Fluttering without a care!
Flowers colourful and bright,
Colourful like a kite!

Long days from morning till night,
Lovely blue sky, there's not a cloud in sight!
Flowers lift their heads for the warmth of the sun,
Children are playing, they are having fun!

Fields ripe with corn swaying in the breeze,
While you are tanning your knobbly knees!
The swallows have flown from far and wide,
To enjoy the summer close by my side.

The ice-cream man earns a lot of money,
Whilst the weather stays fine and sunny.
Autumn is coming as the weather turns grey,
Oh how we long for another sunny day!

Katie Green (11)
Cheadle High School

THAT'S FOOTBALL

I stood there going mad,
My team were really bad,
The manager should be sacked,
His bags they must be packed.

As half-time came and went,
A prayer was duly sent,
But without a single shot,
My team had gone to pot.

Then with the score still at nil-nil,
And all the players were standing still,
The striker who had looked bored,
Surpassed himself and promptly scored.

Oh what a lovely sight,
Celebrations on all night,
But why had we all celebrated?
We'd still been sadly relegated.

Craig Smith (11)
Cheadle High School

HOT AND COLD

Hot things are beautiful
Like fires on cold nights,
Warm summer evenings
When the mood is just right,
The heat from hot dogs
As it warms you right through,
And the breath of a calf
As it gives a small moo!

Cold things are beautiful
Like snow covered mornings,
The little fluffed up robin
As he calls out his warning,
Cool icy drinks
When you've just done a run,
And the crystal-clear ice
Which glistens in the sun.

Jasmin Overton (13)
Cheadle High School

PRECIOUS BEINGS

From seeds you both grew,
And no one ever knew what you would
Look like or even sound or feel like.
And then the time came when you took a breath,
And we loved you.

Anything you do or anything you say is precious
Because you both are precious,
Like a breeze to a bird,
Or water to a fish,
We need you,
And our lives would be nothing without you.

You are my brother and sister,
So fragile and small.
And with the love of us all
You live life to the full
As any child will do,
And I love you.

Richard Lindop (14)
Cheadle High School

JIM

Jim, Jim went for a swim
In the swimming pool,
He got out and dressed himself
And then went off to school.

When at school, Jim sat down,
He did maths and science and French,
The teacher really hated Jim,
So he called her a silly wench.

Jim walked home in the pouring rain,
He was eager to get home,
When he got there he found his house
Had gone to build the Dome.

Debbie Alcock (14) & Anna Harrison (13)
Cheadle High School

THE TRAIN

Moving along,
Ever so strong,
Jumping and thumping.
The smoke turning and curling,
Whirling and purling,
It's battering, clattering,
Shattering and nattering.
It moves along faster and faster,
Louder and louder,
Shouting and screaming,
Growling and squawking.
A great sound as it goes,
Turning, twisting, curling around and around,
With endless rebound.
But then it is quiet,
Just curling and twirling,
Singing and ringing,
On and on it goes.
Till it slows and slows,
Then it stops,
It waits, then,
Moving alone ever so strong.

Nicola Walker (13)
Cheadle High School

THE BONFIRE

It is Bonfire Night at Oakamoor,
There is no entrance or a door,
Just walk in free without a fee.

Hamburgers, beef burgers, hot dogs and chilli,
Teenagers, children and adults being silly,
Bobble hats and scarves and woolly mittens from Nan,
Sparklers at arms length wave as fast as you can.

The fireworks are twizzling and twisting,
Whirling and twirling and popping and dropping,
And sparkling and darkening and shimmering
In the moonlight.

The bonfire is blazing and amazing,
And bubbling and troubling,
And violent then . . . silent.

The people are laughing and joking,
Their feet are clattering and splattering,
And crunching and munching,
And hustling and bustling
As they leave for home.

Hannah Stevens (11)
Cheadle High School

ANIMALS

I think animals are so cute,
Big or large, even minute,
Some stay awake all through the night,
Some may even threaten to bite.

Some are quiet, some are loud,
Some stroll around feeling quite proud,
Some like lying in the sun,
Some just love having fun.

Some have four legs, some have two,
Some say 'Baa', some say 'Moo',
Some are feathery, some are soft,
Some may even live in your loft.

Some are fast, some are slow,
Some like racing to and fro,
Some are always rushing round,
Some love to lie on the ground.

Julie Cooper (12)
Cheadle High School

THE OLD GRAVEYARD

The old graveyard stands still in the day,
But when it's dark and the clock strikes midnight
The spirits let out an evil fright.
Swiftly moving across the cold dark sky,
Wailing and screeching their cry.

They fly across your rooftops,
They pour into your windows.
They go back to their old homes and haunt
The sleeping fellows.

They blow cold chills in your house.
They make your floorboards squeak and crack.
They whisper curses in your ears
And yell out a fear,

Because as soon as the clock crows
They all return to their graves,
And wait for the next night.
So when you're sleeping in your beds
Remember there's spirits above your heads.

Charlotte Rowe (12)
Cheadle High School

MY DOG LUCKY

My dog is fat and small,
Sometimes I remember when he dirtied the hall,
I don't care what anyone says
Because my dear Lucky is better than all the rest!

He has little padded paws
Which patter through the doors,
I don't care what anyone says
Because my dear Lucky is better than all the rest!

He has lots of squeaky toys,
Lucky loves to play with all the girls and boys,
I don't care what anyone says
Because my dear Lucky is better than all the rest!

He's such a sweet little pup,
He loves to be picked up and up!
I don't care what anyone says
Because my dear Lucky is better than all the rest!

I think I'm the one that's *'lucky'*
To have a wonderful, little cutie puppy,
I think Lucky is better than the rest
Because my dear Lucky is the *best!*

Charlotte Brough (11)
Cheadle High School

EXTRAORDINARY WEATHER

I was playing at home,
I saw the lightning flash,
I heard the sky rumble,
Then I heard the thunder crash.

I was going to school,
I stepped in a puddle,
I heard the thunder rumble,
And I thought here comes trouble.

I was in my lessons
I heard the pitter-patter on the windowpane,
I looked out the window,
And it was going down the drain.

I was on my way home
When the rain began to moan.
I felt hailstones
And I began to groan.

I was in my bed,
I saw the lightning flash,
I heard the sky rumble
Then I pulled down the sash.

Jake Jamieson (13)
Cheadle High School

THE WATER SLIDE

A run and a dash,
A smile and a splash,
Giggles and laughs
From everyone near.

First straight and slow,
Fall down sharp,
Off you go.
With a bounce and a pounce,
A swirl and a whirl,
Swirled up and down,
Around and around,
 Quicker and quicker,
Smoother and slicker,
Driving down,
No other sound
But laughing and squealing,
Turning and wheeling,
Showered and sprinkled,
Bubbled and wrinkled,
Turn a last bend,
Come to the end!

Louise Sands (13)
Cheadle High School

DAWN TO DUSK AND THE DARKNESS

The dawn is breaking oh so fast
The morning sunlight appears over the Heavens at last
And in a few hours it's above our heads
The heat of the sun opens the flowers in their beds
It shines all day and it's on the move, on its way
Late afternoon it starts to fade away
Into the sunset it makes its way
As the dusk of the night takes over the sun's array
The moon it rises
And it makes a full appearance in the still of the night
The stars they dance in the sky
If man's wonderful dreams become reality
One day men in spaceships will explore the galaxies.

Andrew Chell (11)
Endon High School

THE REPORT

I opened up the slit,
And stared into the pit
Of what would be my problem.
Instantly I smiled and dropped it in the bin,
'That will get 'em!' I cringed.
They will never know the burning truth,
If they did they'd go through the roof,
But one of them opened it up and looked in to the bin,
'Cor blimey, look what's in the bin.'
'It's a report!' he said.
I caught his eye. 'I'm sorry Dad!' I cried.

David Arthur Ruddle (11)
Endon High School

NEVER MIND

He shall always be remembered,
for his influence on music today.
He didn't care about others' opinions
'Come as you are,' he'd say.

The songs he played reflected his views,
his work was inspiring and original too.
Pressure of fame was too much for him to cope,
for one day he must have abandoned all hope.

He committed suicide, but no one can be sure why,
was it all too much for him? Did he have to die?
And years after, although he has gone and a loss so many will feel,
his music will still always live on.

Sarah Twyford (13)
Endon High School

OOPS!

My friend, her sister and I
Were at the theatre one night,
Her parents had kindly taken us
To see a pantomime.

When intermission came,
Us three, we went downstairs,
We thought we'd play a game
And give her parents a scare!

We hid behind a pillar
And waited quietly
But little did I know,
A surprise was waiting for me!

We heard two sets of footsteps
And jumped out all of a sudden,
But the people we'd scared half to death
Were another couple!

Katie Adams (11)
Endon High School

FOOTBALL FANS

Football is a passionate sport,
With its millions of fans.
They scream and shout for the team they support
And never let them down.

On match day they swarm the stadium
Wearing their team colours,
They glare at the game until someone scores,
Then they either say boo or hooray.

After the game they all go home
Telling their wives the tale.
They're never interested in sport though,
But they still do the same at the next home game.

Sam Dawson (13)
Endon High School

BROTHERS!

As he sits there deeply engrossed
In front of the computer eating toast,
Speeding round on a motorbike
He doesn't think about what I would like,
'Myles homework takes priority
Hurry up or I'll phone the authorities'
'Hang on a second, don't lose your hair
I'll be done in 5 minutes, just wait there.'
'But Myles 5 minutes is just too long,
I'll give you till after this next gong!'
'Or shall we go for a compromise
I'll give you 5 seconds and *no* lies!
5, 4, 3, 2, 1, Myles 5 seconds have just gone'
'Now just get off or I'm phoning Mum!'
'Okay, okay, I'm going away
That's the last race for today!'

Grace Barrett (11)
Endon High School

THE SHED ON WHEELS

We have a shed on wheels
Because my dad's always doing deals.
It goes with a bang and a choke
But it is a bit of a joke.
The back is always smoky
And inside it is a bit pokey.
When we go for a ride
I always make sure I hide.
Soon it's going to be covered in rust
And I'll wake up to a pile of dust -
But I still think my car is a star.

Victoria Rhodes (11)
Endon High School

A POEM ABOUT FOOD

There are many different types of food,
Sweet, sour, delicious and tasty.
Some are bad, some are good,
Sweet, sour, delicious and tasty.

Fruits should be at the top of your list,
Sweet, sour, delicious and tasty.
Cakes should be at the bottom of your list,
Sweet, sour, delicious and tasty.

Some foods are thin, some foods are fat,
Sweet, sour, delicious and tasty.
Some foods are green, some foods are brown,
Sweet, sour, delicious and tasty.

Some foods grow on trees and plants,
Sweet, sour, delicious and tasty.
Also in fields, like corn or wheat,
Sweet, sour, delicious and tasty.

We need our food to keep us alive,
Sweet, sour, delicious and tasty.
If we had no food we all would die,
Sweet, sour, delicious and tasty.

James Thomas (13)
Endon High School

SOUTH PARK POEM

South Park
South Park is the home of Stan Marsh
and his sister Shelly who's big and mean
and very harsh and likes to watch telly.

Further down the road lives Kyle
who always makes you smile.
He's got a little brother named Ike
who everybody's bound to like.

They live near to Kenny who is loved by many.
He's the one who always dies,
Cartman's the one who eats all the fries.
Cartman's the guy who hates to cry
but always managed to eat a pie.
His real name is Eric, say it and he will go hysteric.

So if you're sad and feeling blue
come on down to South Park
it's right for you.

Matthew Smith (14)
Endon High School

MY TRIP TO WALES

I went to Wales
When I was three,
And my little brother
Fell asleep on the potty.

My dad started to film him
While he was asleep,
He started to tip over
But still, he was asleep.

When he woke up
My dad took a photo,
We laughed, he cried,
So of course it was a show.

When we finished laughing
My dad helped him up,
He gave him a drink
In a big round cup.

Louise Pezzaioli (11)
Endon High School

2000!

Two thousand and one
Two thousand and none
Which is the new millennium?
What's all this fuss
That a couple of us
Keep making about which year is which?
When we really should prepare
For this asteroid so rare
That is going to land on the Earth
What asteroid? You say
Well I'll explain if I may
It will come crashing to the floor
Then we'll be no more
Scientists say this
It's a load of tish tish
But I'm still so confused
I've got millennium blues
So this decision is up to you.

Katie Mayer (13)
Endon High School

PREDATOR

Hot, clammy,
The dense rainforest
Is a world of misty humidity.
Shrill shrieks break the silence
As shimmering rainbows of colour fly past.
Vines hang carelessly
In the dark, shadowy depths.
Trees cast pools of dappled light.

Stealthily prowling,
Each sleek sinew taut,
Rosettes rippling,
The deadly predator
Parades into an open glade.
Power emanating from every aggressive pad,
The jaguar, with majestic presence,
Stands alert.

Then, master of the rainforest,
He spies his quarry,
Creeps - then pounces,
Killing his prey with a single, deadly bite.
He seizes his victim -
A lonely hog.
Oblivious of its destiny -
It is no more.

With proud magnificence,
The king of beasts leaves the glade,
Disappearing into thick undergrowth
With straying vines left askew.
Slinking forward,
Jaws firmly gripped,
Oblivious of his destiny,
The noble cat carries the lifeless hog to his lair.

Piercing the silence,
A single, deadly shot explodes through the bush -
Now hushed and still.
Rustling debris sounds an arrival.
Into the glade, another predator
Arrogantly lumbers.
From a pole, the jaguar hangs lifeless,
Once the king of the rainforest - he is no more.

Emma Bentley (13)
Endon High School

MY NEPHEW

Josh is my nephew,
bright and bold.
Playing with toys,
new and old.

I'm always happy,
to play with him.
Racing cars
with firemen in.

His mum is lovely,
one who cares.
She often buys him
teddy bears.

His dad loves him
just as much.
And puts him to bed
with a loving touch.

Darren Parker (13)
Endon High School

ENDON HIGH SCHOOL

I am a new kid at Endon High school,
I sometimes get lost and feel such a fool.

I ask some of the other kids 'Where should I go?'
The older kids look at me and say 'I don't know.'

I hate the pushing and shoving in the corridor,
The noise in the playground is like a roar.

I'm sure I'll never get used to this school,
I sit next to a boy - and that's a rule!

Some of the teachers are nice and kind,
Some of them are strict but I don't mind.

We're here to learn as much as we can,
My form teacher here is a really nice man.

I've made lots of new friends which is really great,
Next year we're going camping and I can't wait.

The cross-country run in PE wore me out,
Some kids are silly and make the teachers shout.

The library is new and full of great books,
If you're noisy in here you get funny looks.

We have homework almost every day,
I go home and get it done, so it's out of the way.

I like Endon High but home time's the best
When I can go home, sit down and have a nice rest.

Elizabeth Williams (11)
Endon High School

A Recipe Poem For A Successful Holiday!

First take 3 over-excited children
And 2 fed up adults.
Cram into a Boeing 757 along with
Several inexperienced hostesses
And 200 impatient people.
Simmer for 2 hours.
Take out passengers and luggage,
Pour into 2 large buses
And transport them to a cockroach-filled hotel.
Whisk up baggage to rooms,
Using a bellboy.
Garnish his hand with a few pesetas
Unpack luggage and pour tired
Passengers into a lilo by the pool.
Allow to simmer under hot sun.
Then cool over a fish supper in
The hotel restaurant.
Slowly marinate in gallon of
Beer and wine.
Then pour tired mixer into large comfortable
Bed and leave overnight.
Serve golden brown holiday makers
2 weeks later.

Katie Belfield (13)
Endon High School

THE BOGART

Upon the Bracken Moorland there sits a Bogart,
Red are his eyes, blue is his body,
He sits with a hunched figure,
Ready to pounce on any unsuspecting visitor who
Might cross his path.

What's this? He hears two people!
Lunch this is, as he thinks to himself,
His big teeth show with a grin as he gets ready
To sink his yellow teeth into human flesh!

As the humans wade and trudge through the
Wet boggy moorland,
The agile Bogart jumps at colossal speed
Over each rock,
Round trees hanging loosely with acres of dead,
Imprinted on their lifeless nature.

A scream of terror as the men see the Bogart,
And the last thing they did see!

If you should ever cross a moor,
And look upon the bog,
Beware because if you should ever blink,
You may never see your life again!

Adam Williamson (13)
Endon High School

I'D LOVE TO HAVE LONG NAILS

I'd love to have long nails, as long as they could be,
I'd love to have long nails, as tall as a tree.
If I could have long nails, I'd polish them every day,
With my long silky hair and peaches and creamy skin,
I'm in the Endon High world.

If my nails were that long I'd break the world record,
Which would get me an award.
Oh what a lot of nail varnish I would have to buy
To see me through the day.

Never mind my dream, I know it won't come true,
But I'm one of those who bites her nails.
So if I could have a little wish that would come true,
I'd love to have my nails as long as a tree,
I'd love to have my nails as long as they can be.

Faye Bibbey (11)
Endon High School

I REMEMBER GRANDAD

I remember that he loved his dog,
I remember that he was lonely,
I remember he liked me very much,
I remember he struggled to look after himself,
I remember he found life hard,
I remember he loved company,
I remember he forgot a lot,
And now I miss him.

Andrew Bradshaw (11)
Endon High School

AUTUMN

Autumn's drawing near again,
And with it comes the fall of rain.
As the wind begins to blow,
The leaves fall to the ground below.
As I gaze outside I wonder,
Will there be storms or thunder?
I watch the leaves twisting and falling,
And hear the wind repeatedly calling.
I run through the leaves, brown and crisp,
The wind whispers loudly as if with a lisp.
Yes, autumn's surely here again,
Spinning round the weather vane.

Rebecca Kelly (11)
Endon High School

WINTER

December is near,
Winter is falling,
Snowflakes are sprinkling past the window,
Icicles are hanging off the shed,
Snow is piling up on the road,
Children sledding down the hills,
Adults doing all their Christmas shopping,
Santa is bringing all the presents,
And New Year is just around the corner.

Louise Adele Butler (11)
Endon High School

COOKIES

With gleaming eyes, eyes of steel
I crept up to the counter.
My praying hands moved up and down,
Not a single skelta.
The jar was around somewhere,
Somewhere on the table.
The sweet smell -
The delicious smell,
My nose was bursting with the smell . . .
Cookies!
Sweet, sweet cookies!
I crave them, I need them,
I want them!
Crack!
'Oh no!' I screamed.
'Nick-las what's going on?'
My belly gibbered - it rippled and boiled.
The cookies were on the floor,
The jar was broken.
'No more cookies for you young lad.'

Nicholas Errington (11)
Endon High School

SCIENCE

From stars in the sky,
To man on the moon,
From aeroplanes,
To space travel.
From LPs
To CDs
      This is a world of science.
From the RAF,
To UFOs.
From Jodrell bank,
To DVD.
From digital TV,
To MTV.
      This is a world of science.
From Magnesium,
To H_2O
From mixing chemicals,
To lighting Bunsen burners.
From learning these,
To remembering them.
      This is my world of science.

Daniel Downing (13)
Haywood High School

OLYMPIC NEWS

Running, weightlifting,
cycling, swimming.
Dive in, go under, swim fast.

Olympic news; she won a gold.
She is happy, smiling,
Cheering, clapping, jumping.

Martyn Lymer, David Gallimore & Daniel Hope (12)
Kemball School

THE FORBIDDEN ATTIC

I open the creaky door,
A single teddy lies forgotten in the corner,
Sad, neglected and alone.
Surrounded by chains is a chest,
I bet there's lots of ancient treasures inside,
Magical and mysterious.

Cobwebs hang from every corner,
Covering secrets yet to be revealed.
Spiders cover the walls of the forbidden attic,
The gloomy room keeps well hidden.

The filthy window shatters as I touch it,
As if it is afraid of me.
I will definitely come back again,
This will be my secret.

Marianne King (11)
Painsley Catholic High School

My Cat

There's something about my cat
The way he acts.
He's asleep on the couch.

His purr is as loud as someone
Using a very, very loud microphone.
His tail flicks like a ring leader's whip.
His fur is as grey as dust,
As soft as cotton.
He wakes up.

As he moves he looks like a tiger.
He goes out.
Outside he frolics in the grass,
Like a baby deer,
And he has no worries!
Sometimes I wish I was my cat,
He's the king of the Close,
Sometimes I wish I was my cat,
My cat Dusty!

Martin Bland (11)
Painsley Catholic High School

School Rush

At six o'clock the alarm bell rings,
It's time to get up and pack my things.
I'm so tired, still half-asleep,
The house is silent, there's not a peep.

I clean my teeth and brush my hair,
It looks a mess but I don't care.
The clock is ticking rather fast,
I don't know how much longer I'll last.

I have my toast and drink my tea,
And open the curtains so I can see.
It's getting late, I must dash,
I must not forget my keys and cash.

I grab my coat and slip on my shoes,
Out the door there's no time to lose.
The bus pulls up outside my door,
I now need to rush no more.

Holly Cheadle (14)
Painsley Catholic High School

AT THE SEASIDE

At the seaside
it's nice and sunny
and there's big waves
that crash against each other
at the seaside there are lots
of seagulls.

There is lots of sand
to play in as well,
if you look carefully
under rocks you will
find crabs.

You can swim in the sea,
the sea goes out and in
at different times.
When the sea goes out at night
the sun sets and
it glows brightly.

John Mills (12)
Painsley Catholic High School

BOB

Meet Bob your average fictional character,
He's not a solider, monk or barrister.
He's made up of five lines, a few squiggles and a head.
Little do you know that he wants everything dead.
That's right he's a stickman, serving time under his driving ban.
Twenty people under his nice, red van.
Even in court he didn't say sorry,
Fleeing the scene in a big hurry.
Harder than most the Grim Reaper in disguise,
He loves to see death, destruction and demise.
His criminal record is huge,
Many blame his childhood of being a stooge.
His favourite death was done by a chainsaw,
Making a huge mess all over the kitchen floor.
He turned to alcohol when he was six,
But still he never forgets to have his Weetabix.
The smell of death, come get a whiff,
In his little world of animated Gif.
So don't look down on this little man,
Don't forget to watch out for his van.
So now say goodbye to him,
It's the chair for Bob, his future's grim.

Dominic Bridgwood (14)
Painsley Catholic High School

THE PENGUIN

Gliding through the water like a dagger,
But then waddling like a duck.
Walking on the freezing ground,
And from the sea the fish he plucks.

Below the freezing moonlight,
He guards the eggs like a very warm nest.
While his partner is out hunting,
He has a very well earned rest!

Hannah Mycock (11)
Painsley Catholic High School

SPEED

The red Ferrari at full throttle,
Will Michael Schumacher keep his bottle?
Approaching Eau Rouge at 200 mile per hour,
His foot to the floor, he can feel the power.
He changes into sixth gear,
The roar of the engine all he can hear.
He takes the first corner; a near perfect line,
Now through the second, he's doing fine.

The approaching pack close in behind,
Another second he must find.
He hits the pedal and off he goes,
Always staying on his toes.
Through the bus stop, and over the line,
Now he's doing just fine.
One more lap that's all to go,
He's not going to lose this one, oh no!
Through the corners one last time,
After this he'll crack open the wine.
Over the line to take the win!
It's Michael Schumacher not the flying Finn!

Jamie Campbell (13)
Painsley Catholic High School

THE MILLENNIUM DOME

The year is nineteen ninety-nine
Tony Blair is Prime Minister
But he said to mark the millennium,
'Let's build a Dome.' Well here's a poem about it.

Tony Blair has hardly any hair
But he said to mark the millennium
'Let's build a Dome.'
'But why?' said the other parties
'Can't we just eat our pie?'
'No, we must keep all the money
Forget about hospitals, forget about the homeless
We will have lots of guests to pay
So think about the pie any day.'
Old Tony Blair said that.
'No, no, no, we must go
We need more hospitals, more homes
Not anymore loans.'
The other parties said that as well
Think once, think twice
Guess what happened
Next the deal was on.
Will London's Millennium Dome be done for the millennium?
Well so it was and what a bodge.
Many people came and went
They all thought it was just a big new tent.
Months went by, it was not to be true.
It was to be sold, but I was told the buyers pulled out
Well they will have to pull it down and waste their money
And think about some more money so they did but in another way.

Rosemary Hall (13)
Painsley Catholic High School

THE MERMAID

By the seaside on a misty night
Adam stood silently watching the waves whirl
The waves crashed at his feet
And on the sandy shore
Adam looked out to sea to see what he could see
On a rock on the horizon
Was a flamboyant figure
Hair as silver as a misty moon
Eyes as blue as a sapphire
Twinkling and sparkling
The figure had not got legs but a tail
A fish tail
Adam had a drink with him
But as soon as he saw the lovely lady
He dropped it in the sparkling sea
And made a splash
As she heard the splash she got scared
And wandered way down to the floor of the sea
Adam rapidly ran along the rocks
And jumped into the wondrous waters
To see where she went
Then all of a sudden *bang*
The mermaid appeared
Again Adam looked in astonishment
At the girl but soon she vanished
Out of sight
Where she went no one knows
But Adam never understood what happened that night
But he never told a soul.

Lucy Wrightson (11)
Painsley Catholic High School

DESTINY OF DEPRESSION

I sit in solitude and look at the life that's passed me by,
Needing the silence to echo around me.
I'm tired of this sadness and desperation,
So swallow me up quiet death.

I'm slipping into depression,
But no one can see.
To all I make this confession,
But there's no one listening to catch me.

There's something inside me,
Tearing away at my blackened soul.
No one can see me,
For the spreading black hole.

Surrounded, in a room full of people.
I'm in the middle but being ignored.
I'm screaming aloud, but no one can hear.
I can feel Depression lurking near.

It's following me, destroying me,
It wants me for its own ends.
I can't escape, contemplating suicide,
I've never been so scared in my whole life.

It controls me, I unwillingly obey,
Angry blood streaming from self-inflicted wounds.
My soul is weak, but I strive to get away.
But I can no longer fight, his I'll be soon.

Savage blood merging with unending tears,
He makes me face my ultimate fears.
He shows me the life that passed me by,
And my destiny of depression, that I can't escape.

Catherine Shaw (15)
Painsley Catholic High School

MY BABY BROTHER

My little baby brother,
So small and so sweet,
His little tiny fingers,
And miniature fat feet,
I look at him in wonder,
He stares at me and smiles,
But then he groans, with one big breath,
He cries.

I change his whiffy nappy and place him in his cot,
Compared to this he's rather small, like a little dot,
I place him in his playroom,
Show him all his toys,
He still doesn't give up,
Why does he make this noise?

I put him in his pushchair and take him for a walk,
I take him to the duck pond, then on the swing,
But nothing stops him crying,
I've tried everything,
I give him his dummy, then his favourite toy,
Which is an ugly baby doll,
Rather silly for a boy.

Then silence, yes he's given up,
I look into his pushchair,
So oblivious without a care,
His small and tender face,
His brown and golden hair,
I take him back home,
He's sweet, without his roar,
Sometimes I stop and giggle,
Dad there's condoms in your draw.

Carly Brunt (14)
Painsley Catholic High School

THE MATCH

The referee blows his whistle,
To signal the start of the game
Stoke are playing a foreign team,
I can't even pronounce their name.

Minutes into the game Mohan pulls down the centre forward
A penalty is awarded to the Croation side,
The striker puts the ball on the spot
But hits it two yards wide.

As Kavanagh runs down the wing
All the crowd start to sing,
Gudjunsson crosses the ball in from the right
Thorne heads it in the net with delight.

The half-time whistle goes
Stoke are winning one none,
The players leave the field
And a streaker runs on.

It's five minutes into the second half
And Thorne is stretched off with an injured calf.
Kavanagh lifts the ball into the box with a flick
Lightbourne finishes with an overhead kick.

The referee blows for full time
The playes leave the pitch,
I'm going down the pub
With my mate Mitch.

Kieran McLoughlin (13)
Painsley Catholic High School

TIDY UP OR BUST

My room is a real pigsty,
Not easy on the eye.
My mum says will you clean it up,
We haven't got a plate or cup.

My mum installed a height chart,
To measure up the mess level.
It's rising way above the mark,
They'll be shouting like the devil!

A danger sign is on the door,
Hard hats here, a must.
There's little hope of seeing the floor,
It's tidy up or bust!

Swings and pulleys aid my flight,
From bed to door in the dead of night.
All forms of peril lurk about,
The danger sign you shouldn't flout.

I enter now at massive risk,
A tidy room about to fix.
I'll do it with no safety net,
I know you think I can't I bet.

I could be gone for quite some time,
But I'll be back - please don't pine.
I hope to see you all once more,
That's if dad don't seal the door.

Joanna Parry (14)
Painsley Catholic High School

POEM ON CREATION

Day 1 - The first day was cold and dark, nothing to be seen,
Then suddenly God said, 'Let there be light,'
There was light a big beam.
God said that this was good and seperated light from dark,
He called light day and dark night, so night was dark and
day was bright.

Day 2 - Then God said let there be expanse between water and water,
The top is sky and the bottom is sea,
I have created two things how clever of me.

Day 3 - Then God said, let the sea be gathered in all one place,
Parts are called land and parts are called sea,
That is the world at its base,
Produce food for all the people as well as can be.

Day 4 - Then God said let there be sun and moon,
Sun for day and moon for night
And also let there be stars,
So people will see a pretty sight.

Day 5 - Then God said let the sea be filled with living things
And the air be filled with birds,
These things happened as God spoke his words.

Day 6 - Then God said let there be human beings,
To look after my fish, plants and animals and all that I have created,
But most of all, look after yourselves, love one another and never
be hated.

Day 7 - God rested.

Leanne Baylay (13)
Painsley Catholic High School

IF . . .

If there's a God why is there so much hurt?
Why have some got so much and others not even a shirt?

If there's a God why is there so much hate,
And whether you live or die is down to fate.

If there's a God why does money rule?
It makes some people horrible and cruel.

If there's a God why are some children abused?
This leaves me shocked and confused.

If there's a God why is the Earth polluted so much?
Why doesn't he stop it with just one touch?

If there's a God why is there war and fighting,
And why are people struck down by lightning?

If there's a God why do some people have no water,
And why are innocent animals led to slaughter?

If there's a God why do accidents happen each day,
Surely he didn't want things to turn out this way?

If there's a God why do I feel like this,
Am I right to think that the fault is all his?

If there's a God I ask with all my heart,
For all the hatred in our world to depart.

If there's a God I ask him with glee,
All the people suffering please, set them free.

So if there's a God the question I ask until the day I die . . .

Plain and simple that question is *why?*

Laura Delaney (12)
Painsley Catholic High School

SCHOOL!

Beep, beep, beep my alarm clock rang,
Time to get up!
My mum cheerfully sang.
I fell out of bed half asleep,
But in my head,
I was still counting sheep.
Oh I sighed not another day at school,
I haven't done my homework,
I will look a fool!
I slammed the front door in a bad mood,
Bye Mum!
I unhappily booed.
I waited at the bus stop freezing cold,
When the bus rolled up,
All rusty and old.
I could see the school building over the hill,
I stepped off the bus
And felt a sudden chill.
I glanced at my watch, I was 10 minutes late,
I ran into class
And discovered my fate.
You're late again the teacher bawled,
Tee, hee, hee!
Someone called.
I sat in my chair,
I was thinking,
It's not at all fair.
Why do we have to go to school,
I didn't do my homework,
I did look a fool!

Laura Hancock (13)
Painsley Catholic High School

HALF-PAST THREE

Friday afternoon is finally here,
I thought it would never come,
I wish the day would end,
Quarter-past three I'm sitting here,
Waiting for half-past three to come.

The clock is ticking,
Tick, tock, tick,
But the hands don't seem to move,
Please time hurry up,
I want to go home.

I'm listening to the teacher,
Waiting to hear 'Pack away!'
But it's only twenty-past three
Ten more minutes I have to wait
Be patient time will come.

Twenty-five past three,
The day is drawing to an end,
I'm watching, waiting, trying to keep calm,
One minute to go!

I frantically pack away my pencil case and books,
For half-past three is eventually here,
I run out of the room with a cheer,
Cause half-past three is the time.

School has finished,
I thought it never would,
I run to the bus as fast as I can,
No school tomorrow,
I can stay in bed,
Cause half-
past three came and went.

Sarah Flackett (13)
Painsley Catholic High School

WINTER

As autumn comes to a dreary end,
Winter emerges from its depths.
The icy sharpness in the air,
The bitter feeling which you cannot compare.
A glacial blast drifts over my face,
My fingers too frigid to tie my lace.
The snow on the hills like a blanket on a bed,
My scarf wrapped tightly around my head.
The naked trees, a frozen lake,
This bitter chilliness is not fake.
My breath turns into a cloud of white,
The sun is blocked, there is no light.
The land is still, dull and dark,
The tree's protection, a coat of bark.
Animals taking refuge from the cold,
The icy grip takes its hold.
My toes are frozen in my shoes,
These sub-zero temperatures we'd like to lose.
The bright ball in the sky has gone,
I try and find warmth but there is none.
Hands are rubbed furiously together,
When will we see the end to this awful weather?
Snowflakes falling to the ground,
Snowballs are made nice and round.
When these winter months disappear,
It won't be long again before they are here.

Adam Brunt (14)
Painsley Catholic High School

DREAMS

Last night as I lay in my bed
I dreamt a dream in my head,
It all started spinning,
As though I was flying,
I fell in a room with a thud.
A statue of me there stood,
I looked around the gigantic hall,
On the floor was a great big ball,
From the window it was bewitching
The sea, the sand and three bears dancing
I stepped outside onto the beach,
The waves crashing at my feet.
I walked around my island fair
And everything was in a pair.
I found someone just like me
Sitting in an enormous tree.
We went walking and found a forest,
Even bigger than my sisters closet.
The forest was enchanting,
With trees, lakes and rainbows.
Like something from a fairy tale.
Out of the lake came a whale,
Then it all began to fade,
The little world I had made,
From afar I heard a cry,
Something about a fly,
All of a sudden I woke up fast,
My clock said 25 past,
It all seemed so real to me,
It all still will at half-past three.

Alyx Tipper (13)
Painsley Catholic High School

PUNISHMENTS

The detention room was silent,
no one dared to move.
The punishments at the school were violent,
as if they had something to prove.

The teachers rarely did shout,
but each was armed with a cane.
They would often give you a forceful clout,
and make you cry with pain.

Pages of lines you'd have to write,
and graffiti cleaning and litter picking.
The end of detention seemed never to be in sight,
and the hands on the clock just carried on ticking.

Mrs Barns with her hands by her side,
would creep around the classroom and watch us read.
She would reach for her cane if anyone cried,
and crack it down on their hand with phenomenal speed.

The school building looked grim,
no one ever came near.
No wonder there weren't many children there,
at a school so violent and full of fear.
Why couldn't the punishments have been more fair?

Sarah Wright (14)
Painsley Catholic High School

A View To A Death

Life's greatest fear of all is death
It will happen to all of us eventually
The scary thing is, we don't know when
Some may choose to die, others love to live

Death is an eerie concept
No one knows what it's like to die
There's no one to give you advice
No reassurance that there's life after death

Who knows if there is a heaven
Who knows if there is a hell
Truth is, no one knows for sure
And that is the thing that frightens the most

Perhaps when you're in heaven
It's a whole new experience
You can look down upon the living
Relations, or talk to past ancestors

The phobia exists, but my final thought is this
It may be a reformation
To farewell the world with a final kiss
And elevate to a new karma
To live as one with rigor mortis.

James Rathmell (15)
Painsley Catholic High School

THE TEACHER

She sits on her chair
Running her fingers through her hair,
Her face so grin,
But she's got a big hairy chin.

At her desk, she commands,
With her voice and her hands,
At the end of the day she has swollen glands.

By dinner time
We've got a rhyme,
It's all about her,
But my friends would not concur.

They say it's too harsh,
But I don't care,
I just want to laugh
And raise her hair.

By the end of the day,
We've all had a play,
She's on her last legs,
She can't stand the boys
And she hates our toys,
When the bell goes
She stands on her toes and bellows
'Out of my sight!'

Adam Stephens (14)
Painsley Catholic High School

ETERNAL HISTORY

Fame and fortune,
What shall it be?
Fame or fortune,
Which one's for me?

Fame is but a word,
Simple mans decree,
The meaning is unknown to us,
Its farce a travesty.

Fortune blesses those,
Those with energy,
The fame it gains,
Shame it contains,
Where once was truth, now lies.

Who needs popularity?
I'll sit here all alone,
Rocking, craving, thinking,
Of things I'll never own.

Who really needs either?
Perhaps we'll wake to see,
That life is but a query
And not a mystery.

Ewan Brock (15)
Painsley Catholic High School

MACBETH

The witches are the ones you'll see,
Casting spells of red and green,
The colours that will shout out loud,
Because they're so vivid and so proud
To be evil and unkind,
To those who have an innocent mind.

They circle the cauldron and shout out loud;
'Hubble, bubble, toil and trouble,
Fire burn and cauldron bubble,'
Making spells to cause you pain,
Shout out for help, but all in vain,
As you tumble down the spiral stair,
To an evil life, which you despair
To see your end with gruesome flare,
You'll know it's over when you get there.

So take my advice
And steer well clear,
Of misty heaths,
On treacherous nights,
I know myself, that I should have done,
Then I wouldn't be here and still not have won,
The throne that the king sits upon.

Sarah Wright (14)
Painsley Catholic High School

FOUR-LEAVED CLOVER

Life is a mystery;
A prodigias game to play.
You throw a dice -
Hold your head up high
And wish for a happy day.

Back a space: Two steps forward
In how the game goes.
Each day is precious
Hold to it tight,
Smile away those woes.

Which direction will you take?
It's really up to you;
Remember every day starts afresh
Bright, hopeful and a-new.

Things will go wrong from time to time
And down that ladder you will fall.
Climbing it again is a must
Prove the world - you stand tall!

The game is quick - it's almost over,
Was that really it?
Your life has just passed you by,
Did you find your four-leaved clover?

Emma Hackney (14)
Painsley Catholic High School

TIGER

Tiger lying in the light of day,
Hears humans coming, wakes and slinks away,
Object of universal fright,
Prowling creature of the night.

Crawling through the bushes or the grass,
An elongated, deadly, killing mass,
Patterned with stripes that are the darkest black,
Interspersed with fiery orange on his back.

The total of varieties make a count of eight,
But are all now endangered at a fast increasing rate,
Bengal, Chinese, Caspian, Javan,
Indo-Chinese, Balinese, Siberian, Sumatran.

Their range of land is shrinking,
And their numbers quickly sinking,
Men hate them for the theft
Of the only prey that's left.

This prey is the herds intruding their home,
The animals that man likes to claim as his own,
Hunting, logging and farming have caused tigers distress,
And only man, their enemy, can save them from this mess.

The Balinese tigers are today all gone,
But if we co-operate we can right our previous wrong,
If we stop persecuting, the tigers and their prey,
Then the tiger nation will survive past today.

Julie Wooldridge (13)
Painsley Catholic High School

POVERTY

Every day's a struggle,
Every day's a strive.
A constant fight for survival,
A battle to stay alive.

The wild winds blow so coldly,
There's rain and hail and snow.
The outside world's so dark and dull,
But there's nowhere else to go.

They live in destitution,
No possessions, money or home.
No one seems to notice,
That they are all alone.

They require help for survival,
They need mercy, help and aid,
To stay alive, to live each day,
With our help, they can be saved.

They have much less than we do,
We take it all for granted.
There's those who are less fortunate.
A chance is all they want.

When the day closes its curtains
And the night time breeze blows through,
They're out there waiting hopefully,
Needing help for you.

Natalie Smith (16)
Painsley Catholic High School

THE ZOO SCHOOL TRIP

They mentioned the word 'zoo',
When I went to the staff meeting,
My poor little heart nearly stopped beating.

With last year,
I'd had it up to the brim,
Because the children are simply so dim.

It snowed on the day,
We decided we wouldn't go.
The children started screeching, so we said 'Okay let's go.'

We eventually arrived there,
I took a deep breath
And prepared to have a long, painful death.

'Eric!' I screamed,
As he entered the cage,
The sabre-tooth tiger went in a terrible rage.

'Claire!' I then cried,
'Don't put your hand in that poo,
And Johnny, please get off that kangaroo.'

'Harriet!' I shrieked,
'Put down that snake!'
She ran off in tears, she had thought it was fake.

So I was glad,
When they said we had to go,
I'd had enough and never would have said no.

So I decided,
Before next year's trip comes around,
I'm taking early retirement!

Sarah Clowes (15)
Painsley Catholic High School

THOSE YEARS

I'm younger than my sister,
And believe it when people say,
Growing up is awful,
My sister gives that away.

On her 14th birthday,
It hit me suddenly,
When she ran straight upstairs,
And would not come down for tea.

She turned her music up so loud,
It made the floor vibrate,
Puberty was in process,
Her bad temper couldn't wait.

She demands proper lingerie now,
And is growing by the minute,
The old crop top is redundant,
Now her bra's got something in it.

'What colour next?' Mum sighs,
She had such lovely hair,
Now it's spiked and greasy,
And sprouting everywhere.

All sweet and bright today,
Tonight she's acting coy,
Dad shouts, 'Back by ten!'
He knows she's seeing that boy.

What will I do? How will I cope?
The thought leaves me quite heady.
'Now don't worry love,' mumbled Mum,
'You're halfway there already!'

Vanessa Rowlinson (14)
Painsley Catholic High School

CAROL'S DAY OUT

(Based on 'Our Day Out' by Willy Russell)

I walk past the gnome with carrier bag in hand,
We are going on a trip, which Mrs Kay has planned.
I am wearing my scruffy uniform that I wear every day,
For school, eating, travelling and play.

In my desperate urge to get to school,
I nearly got ran over, Les said I was a fool!
When I finally got there, I was ready to go,
Where? I hear you ask, that I don't know!

Travelling along on the coach, what a thrill,
I can tell this trip is going to be brill!
We stopped at a shop, and I got something to eat,
Next we stopped at a zoo, what a treat!

Conway Castle which we thought was our last stop,
But no, we went to the beach right at the top.
I love it here, it is the best place ever,
If I had the choice to leave I would say *'Never!'*

But we didn't leave without going to the fair,
I had the best time, without a care.
My face dropped when we had to go back home,
Back to my house with the garden gnome.

Victoria Bell (13)
Painsley Catholic High School

THROUGH THE AGES

A million dreams, a million thoughts,
For these, our minds are like cages.
Dreams of spaceships, pirates, highwaymen,
Of bands playing on great stages.
So if you find you have these too,
You're travelling through the ages.

Moving on, trying to catch the world,
But your history written in pages.
You have a family of four, no car,
You're working in a job that pays bad wages.
You've got to run fast just to catch up,
You're living through the ages.

You try your best, but it can't be helped,
You go faster anyway,
All the things you have in your life,
You wish they'd only stay.

Dreams are made of thoughts,
Thoughts are made of dreams.
Walking through the ages,
Running through the ages,
Falling through the ages,
Crawling through the ages.

Chris Morton (15)
Painsley Catholic High School

THE GIFT

The tiny child had been born,
her first breath was like trying to catch the
howling wind with her bare hands.
Her imperceptible limbs were like blocks of ice
wriggling and twitching in the air.
A soft cloud like a blanket floated, soon
surrounding her body, melting her blocks of ice.
Towering above her were two mountains.
The air soon appeared warm and cosy,
opening her beautiful blue stars she
peered over the cloudy blanket
to the people whom had put her there,
she was a gift, a tremendous gift.
And a true gift she was.

Megan Byatt (12)
Painsley Catholic High School

A SCARY THING!

This is a thing that can scare you witless,
It looks down on death, demons and witches.
It sets you tasks that you don't want,
And makes you sweat and shiver.
The sight of it would turn anything white,
And give the most fearless man a blooming good fright.
Its punishment would make anyone yearn,
As it keeps you in Hell for eternity.
It makes you do things to numb anyone's mind,
And this frightening dreaded thing I'm talking about?
Well it's the teacher - of course!

Ross Daniels (11)
Painsley Catholic High School

MY BIKE

On my bike, my feet clip in, ripping along,
I come to a cliff, my brakes are screeching,
Scraping, grinding, gritting spitting,
Down the cliff I am hammering,
My bike goes twang, clonk, clang,
Off the cliff, whistling, smooth, the silent . . .
The crunch, snap, smash, lash,
Front wheel burning, tyre is squirming,
Brakes are cracking, spokes are twanging,
Getting smoother, my bum is bruised,
With a clank and a churn my bike begins to burn,
The last big bump, splash, into a rocky river.
Wicked!

Francis Swinnerton (12)
Painsley Catholic High School

UNTITLED

What a horrible class I'm in,
Liam's loopy, Paul always picks his nose,
And Claire always cries,
But then there are some cool people like my friends,
Dangerous Dan for instance,
He's always got a smile on his face,
But the others you can't see a smirk in sight,
The other day we went on a plane,
We were gliding through the air,
Back on land with a *bang!*
We crashed, now we've got broken bones
So it's time out from the dreaded school
Yeah!

Joseph Hurst (11)
Painsley Catholic High School

HOPE

Enveloping the night and the day,
The eerie shadow invaded the way.
The sun vanished and no more was there light,
Instead was the darkness they called 'night.'

The clouds shifted from my sight,
I lost my reach to their great height.
Stars glistened against the dark blanket of gloom,
Contrasting the darkness, they shone with the moon.

In the dark, I tried to scope,
The star that managed all my hope.
But my star, my hope, was out of gain,
Leaving me alone with all my pain.

Laura Houldcroft (15)
Painsley Catholic High School

WAR - THERE'S NO POINT

My nan always tell me about the war
The dreaded sound of the battle's roar,
But to myself I'm always thinking
What is the point of war?

The war carries on, on land, air and sea,
But why do they have to disagree?
So many people get injured and killed,
There is no point in war.

I try to escape but then there's more
I am forever hearing the sound of war
Why don't people agree with me
That there is no point in war.

Gerard Scheuber (14)
Painsley Catholic High School

THE FIRST DAY!

I walked up to the big school gate,
I looked at my watch, I was five minutes late,
I started to run, the wind in my face,
Oh no! Would I make it? I was in such a state.

My classroom was there, I wish I was home,
Wrapped up in my bed, all on my own,
I opened the door, everybody turned to look,
I mumbled 'I'm sorry' and got out my book.

The clock hit three-thirty,
I could hardly wait,
To get out of here,
Walk out the big school gate.

Lisa Rafferty (13)
Painsley Catholic High School

MY GRANDAD

I love to stay on Grandad's farm
Upon the Yorkshire moors
Although he talks rather odd
Like 'Shut them there doors.'

He sometimes takes me fishing
And when I catch a trout
'Ey that's grand lad'
Is what he's heard to shout!

'Up the wooden hill for you
- time to go to bed'
He's always looking after me
Yorkshire born and bred!

Carl Machin (12)
Painsley Catholic High School

THE MILLENNIUM DOME

The Dome, the Dome,
There's nothing like it,
Some people say it's a good day out,
Others say we'd rather be without,
Some are angry,
Because it's so costly.
Others are rightly proud of our bounty.
It's gone bust,
It's not robust.
But whatever we way,
Blair says 'Tis here to stay!'
So how long will it last?
When will its time be past?
What will we build by 3000?
Will the dome be dust or legend?
Perhaps we will be living on Mars,
Driving rockets, instead of cars.

Matthew Capper (11)
Painsley Catholic High School

HELPLESS

The waves crashed over the cliffs,
Pulling back into the choppy waters,
Taking with them a man from the shore.
Spluttering and splashing desperately he tried to
Free himself from the ocean's grip.
It was like a child cruelly playing with a hamster!
The sea opened its mouth, and swallowed him.
There was nothing we could do,
He was gone!

Shannon Vasey (12)
Painsley Catholic High School

DEATH ROW

Dead man walking, dead man walking,
A new face enters death row.
A tall, grim man, into the padded cell.
One, two, three weeks gone and it's time to walk.
Down the last mile, he walks and walks,
Then he reaches the electric chair, his head bald and bare.
Any last requests, 'No!' he replies.
He is seated down and strapped in,
His time is up it is time to die.
The famous last words are said to his face,
Electricity will be passed through your body,
Until you are dead, throw on one,
Throw on two, silence.
Next week we will do it all again, and again,
And again, and after each one there will be . . .
Silence.

Ben Cornwall (12)
Painsley Catholic High School

AUTUMN

Cooling breezes past my ears,
I can see my breath as I speak.
Leaves are falling just like tears.
Flowers hang their heads,
Gardens look bleak.

Evening comes quickly, darkness falls.
Autumn is here, nature's ready to sleep.
The birds gather to leave our shores.
Summer sun has gone,
But memories we can keep.

Francesca Brown (12)
Painsley Catholic High School

A CAT!

Ever since I was young I longed for a cat.
A black cat, a ginger cat, a tabby cat at that.
A cat to cherish and cuddle and comfort and stroke.
A cat to cradle, cocooned in a huge cosy cloak.

A cat with deep green and sparkly eyes
That would glow and illuminate in the dead of the night.
A cat with a coat and a purr made of silk.
A hungry cat to nourish with a saucer of milk.

A cat that would grin as it sat on my lap
Curled up so comfy for its afternoon nap.
A cat that would meet me as I got through the door.
A cat I could pet, love and adore.

Ever since I was young, a longed for a cat.
A black cat, a ginger cat, a tabby cat at that.
A cat that was carefree, charming and cheery.
A cat that was clever, cheeky and chirpy.

Claire Richards (15)
Painsley Catholic High School

NIGHT SKY

The stars glimmer
And sometimes glow.
When the sleepers lie on their beds below,
This is what the moon will show.

As the light reflects upon the ground,
The shooting star makes a sound.
Into oblivion goes the light
Farewell to all of the night.

Jack Woolley (13)
Painsley Catholic High School

LITTLE RED RIDING HOOD - THE TRUTH

I bet you've heard the story where,
Red Riding Hood's sweet with curly blonde hair.
But here's the truth, so better beware,
So to keep out of her way you'd better take care.
Red Riding Hood was a real bad babe,
(Or Bernie as she's known,)
She got around with all the lads,
She was never on her own.
She drew them in, like moths to flame,
Awaiting certain death.
Death by Bernie, was what it was called,
It left you out of breath.
And what of the wolf (I hear you cry),
Why, he was nothing but a bloke,
He seemed to have never heard of fun,
He converted Bern, she saw the light,
And now poor Bern's a nun.

Lucy Malcolm (14)
Painsley Catholic High School

MY ONE WISH

If I could have one wish of all,
I'd have mountains of chocolates wall to wall.
It would cover the houses and line the streets,
Chocolate everywhere for me to eat.
The creamy chocolate, dark, milk and white,
It would be so delicious I'd eat every last bite.
The trees, the roads and buildings too,
I'd eat the sweet chocolate, but nothing for you.
I would chomp my way around the city,
There'd be nothing left, oh what a pity!

Avril Taylor (13)
Painsley Catholic High School

I Used To Wish I Was Popular...

I used to wish I was popular,
I used to wish to be cool,
I used to wish to be one of them,
And not seem such a fool.

Now I'm glad I am not popular,
Now I am glad I am not cool,
Now I am glad I am not one of them,
'Cause they are the real fools.

The friends they have are many,
The friends I have are few,
They acted really cool,
And I felt like such a fool.

I used to wish to be popular,
I used to wish to be cool,
I used to wish to be one of them
And not seem such a fool.

Now I am glad I am not popular,
Now I am glad I am not cool,
Now I am glad I am not one of them,
'Cause they are the real fools.

The friends they have are many,
The friends I have are few,
But the friends they have are fake
And the friends I have are true.

They think they are popular,
They think that they are cool,
They think we want to be one of them,
Ha, they are such fools.

The friends they have are fake,
Ours are true,
And are very cool!

Joanna Handy (14)
Painsley Catholic High School

A POEM FOR WEDNESDAY

A poem for Wednesday
The middle of the week
Sitting there blankly
Can't be bothered to speak.
Yet later blooms Friday
The weekend is in sight
A chance for euphoria
Paying visit to the night.
Saturday morning glory
Pressure and ease divide
Varying from Wednesday
Where I prefer to hide.
Exhaustion by Monday
Sunlight blinding your eyes
Thoughts quickly disappear
Released into the skies.
Praying for happiness
Mountains to climb
A poem for Wednesday
At least it will pass the time.

Steve Long (15)
Painsley Catholic High School

THE STATUE

Sitting, soaking up the sun
Skin a lovely golden brown
His hat a copper, laced with gold
Still and silent, quiet all around.

Sitting, dripping in the rain
Skin a shiny, peachy lake
Drip, drop, splish, splash
Still and silent, never a sound.

Sitting, covered in fallen leaves,
Red and yellow, and green and brown
Never moving to throw them off
They create a blanket, 3 feet deep.

Sitting, covered, in the snow,
Glistening, sparkling, shimmering white
Buried in the soft white blanket
Never a moment, never a word.

Our person is a statue bronze
Sitting silent all year around
Non-breathing, non-living
He'll live for ever and ever and more.

Samantha Davey (15)
Painsley Catholic High School

SPRINT

'On your marks'
My heart beats, will I win?
Faster, faster! Thud thud!
It's a gold medal if I win and come first!
'Bang'
The starter gun fires,
I push off, my legs start moving
'Go on you can do it!'
My supporters shout and scream my name.
They rely on me to gain another gold.
I sprint the fastest I've ever run,
I turn my head 45°
I'm winning . . .
50 metres . . . 60 metres . . .
The finishing line comes into view!
My heart rate gets faster,
I dip my neck and cross the line first.
I won! I won! I'm Olympic champion!
The crowds scream my name.
I wap my national flag around my shoulders.
The press take my picture,
It appears all over tomorrow's news.

Suzannah Cordon (13)
Painsley Catholic High School

WINTER

Winter starts off with rain
Everyone thinks I wish it was summer again.
It gets colder and chillier
The rain gets heavier
Until it turns to sleet.

The middle of winter
The sleet keeps falling
But gets thicker as it comes
Loud crashes of the sleet on the roofs
The thickness goes . . .

The end of winter is . . .
Silence
The sleet is all gone
There is nothing to be heard
The great fall of the snow

The ground is covered
In an ice-white carpet
The proper winter
Is here once more.

Winter.

Lauren Tilstone (11)
Painsley Catholic High School

OPTIONS

(The fear of growing up)

The decisions that require me to answer,
Seem to multiply faster each day,
I deliberate over the reasons,
Just to conclude with an 'if' or a 'may'.

I've seen many people before me,
Take the task that I face in their stride,
Yet for me it seems,
As though all of my dreams,
Go out of their way,
To lead me astray,
And conflict my desire to decide.

They advise and instruct and forewarn,
That our future is coming up fast,
But I'd rather sit back and observe,
And worry when choosing is past.

Now the boxes with trepidation are ticked,
Like the envelope, my fate I have sealed,
I'm to be thrown in the deep end to find,
What my destiny, unjustly concealed.

Laura Parry (15)
Painsley Catholic High School

THE FOLLOWER

When I see you, I am destined to follow
But such is the terror that you might realise
That I shrink back, engulfed in non-description
And I melt, gushing silently through the hall
The fault is with you, your entrusted perfection
Every inch is emblazoned, like fire in my mind
I know all that exists, and all that has been
About you: you are my corruption, my sensuous study
You manipulate me innocently, make me creep and shift
From place to place, around you, by you, with you
But never daring to venture into your circumference
For you might see me - might pierce me with vision
And then, it would be over - my nightmare would end
My thoughts forbidden, eternally condemned to secrecy
All my radical hopes torn jaggedly to shreds
And my nightmare would be over, over
But if my fears are diminished, how can I live?
If you took my cup of desperation from me
I would not, could not, have life, have death -
I would be nothing. Without you I am nothing
For I must always follow, follow
Follow you.

Lucy Woolliscroft (15)
Painsley Catholic High School

WHAT WOULD HAVE BEEN?

Precious are the times spent with family and friends,
That relationships past, we are unable to mend.
I wonder what would be, if I had of done that,
If my life would have changed, if I hadn't just sat,
If my hidden euphoria and chances unknown,
Had not stayed the same but blossomed and grown,
If I'd have gone left, rather than right,
If I'd not given in, but put up a fight,
If the night had not ended, if you hadn't walked away,
If I could have stopped just one more day,
If I'd stood on the table and proclaimed out loud,
My feelings for you I'd kept hidden in shroud,
If you'd turned around and looked into my eyes,
If we hadn't had to say our goodbyes,
If I'd taken the chance when it was given to me,
Instead of hesitating with uncertainty,
If I had the choice would I do it again
And be wondering now if it's worth the pain?
If I'd have done things without thinking first,
Would life have turned out for the worst?
And still I sit with things I've not seen,
Still asking myself - 'What would have been?'

Nicola Collier (16)
Painsley Catholic High School

MATRIARCH OF BLADES

Malicious and evil is the person I wish not to know.
Oblivious to the pain and anguish, she has undoubtedly caused.
Hurting so many people without even realising.
Her thoughtless, callous actions I will never cease to forget.
A permanent scar of hate replaces what was once pure love.
What drove her to such destruction?
Why did she see this as her only way out?
A caring hand could have protected her, offering guidance.
Instead a path of pain was chosen
And to reject her devoted family

Every day I wonder how she continues to live,
Realistically I know I will never be able to forgive.

Esther Porter (15)
Painsley Catholic High School

LIFE'S A GREAT MYSTERY

Life is a great mystery,
Some people live, some people die,
Whether we want them to or not,
We always end up wondering why.

The rain will fall and the sun will shine,
Some people laugh and some people cry,
Some people always smile
But whatever happens everybody will always hurt inside for a while.

We try to get things to complete our life,
Friends, family, husband or wife,
But whatever happens we try and it never seems to work,
'Cause life's a mystery, such a great mystery!

Laura Rigby (14)
Painsley Catholic High School

LEARNING TO DRIVE

The clutch goes in and the gear is changed,
I look out of the window, my face looks pained.
The car starts to jump, we swerve to the side,
My heart skips a beat, thankfully the road's wide.
Some knobs are turned, the fans blow cold air,
Goose bumps appear and it's messed up my hair.
The accelerator's down, the car flies on,
The likelihood of crashing is second to none.
My teeth are clenched, my knuckles show-white,
I grip the seat, no future in sight.
I start to worry, will I see another day?
I'm forced to the right, we're going the wrong way!
I look forward and am ashamed to see,
The driver is my sister Stephanie.

Sarah Wilks (16)
Painsley Catholic High School

INSANITY

Lost and helpless in a haze of voices,
But she can't deciphere a single sound,
Her mind an entanglement of unknown fears,
Choked and suppressed from the world around,
An endless swirl of confusion and chaos,
Seeing faces that aren't really there,
Stalked by the memories of her own haunting past,
Hidden away from the people who care,
Standing on the fringe of insanity,
Past the point of no return,
Frenzied feelings of disturbing perceptions,
Her darkened world of mistrust and concern.

Laura Campbell (15)
Painsley Catholic High School

FRIENDSHIP

Friendship, I think, can never be replaced,
It's the friendship in this world,
That makes it a wonderful place.

Friends can talk to each other,
Keep secrets and jokes,
That's why friends love and care for each other,
Like sister and brother,
Even though they have their ups and downs.

Friends have loads of fun,
They sing and shout and mess about.
That's why you can never tear best friends apart,
Because friendship, is always in their hearts.

Katie Withington (13)
Painsley Catholic High School

SORROW

The anguish she felt could never be explained
For the Elysian tranquility was completely stained
Secluded was she from the life they once led
Remembering the fickle words which she once said:
'Everything in life offers a meaning
It isn't there to cause sorrowful feelings'
Now she had knowledge that this wasn't true
Having had experienced what misery can do
Visible were the scars left by her pain
Disillusion was what she had gained
Everything was lost, not a hope to save
As she looked down on her husband's grave.

Cora Moodie (15)
Painsley Catholic High School

THE ALARM CLOCK
(Inspired by my morning - 2nd October 2000)

I groan aloud as my ears begin ringing,
Beside me the dratted alarm clock is singing,
Thus emerging from my slumber, I am confused,
Then as realisation kicks in, I am not amused,
The reverberating drone resounding through the air,
Forces me to smack it - hence the worse for wear,
Alas, to no avail, the howling never ceases,
And so I am driven to tear it to pieces,
Eventually it retreats, into 'silent state'
Waiting for a time to again force me awake
For now I drift back, into my paradise world,
Where I lie under duvet, with the sheets unfurled,
The offensive timekeeper haunts me every morn,
Rousing me from deep sleep at the break of dawn,
As you can see I am not a morning person,
Due to finding the rude awakening irksome.

Katie Stanier (15)
Painsley Catholic High School

THE OPPOSITE POEM

Heavy as a brick,
Light as a feather,
Fat as a sumo wrestler,
Thin as a stick,
Hard as a willow,
Soft as a pillow,
Strong as a wrestler,
Weak as a bird.

I am a bull.

Matthew Hurst (11)
Painsley Catholic High School

MY BEST OBJECT

My best object is something with a mouse
many people might have one in their house
it is very small
but to some quite tall
some cannot live without it
some don't know anything about it
you can crack codes
and set different modes
it can be entertaining
it can give your brain a training
it gives you an advantage with homework
it can make a digital clock work
some can play a DVD
it can make a picture 3D
some can run a TV channel
some can run a voting panel
here's a big clue to help you
it's a computer.

Darren Grzesiak (12)
Painsley Catholic High School

INFANTS

I   nfants are a pain, they bawl, they bellow, they scream.
N ever giving a second thought to where they may be seen.
F   orever being destructive and ruining all my things,
A nd when they try to sing . . .
N o one is left to hear the roaring, wailing, ping.
T   o end my infants poem, I will say one thing,
     Don't have an infant it's a terrible thing.
S   hhhhh!

Charlotte Randall (11)
Painsley Catholic High School

DAYTIME

The light of the sun gleaming,
Day has come.
The sun like a fire alight in the sky.
I look out of my window,
And see the flowers open.
It is the day of the summer.
I go upstairs and put my shorts on to go outside.
The brightness of the sun hurts my eyes.
The sea splashing against the sand,
This is the best place to be,
Sunbathing on a beach in Spain.
Life can't get much better than this.
I can see the sun rays on the sea,
I am getting a rather good tan
My face glowing brightly,
How can I ever say that life isn't fair?

Jennifer Keeling (11)
Painsley Catholic High School

DIRTY TOES

Me un me mate
Fought it'd be dead funny
To go up Anley
When it wer sunny,
An' 'ave a laugh,
Un make everyone think,
That they really did
Stink!
So we'd 'old us nose,
So they'd think they smell like dirty toes!

Francesca Talbot (12)
Painsley Catholic High School

WIND

Stinging, chilling
Pushing people around.
Dashing through the leaves
My breath being taken away
By the big windy breeze.

Blastering, blustering,
Shooting through the trees.
Diving, curling over the branches,
Gasping for air as it blows through my hair.
Touching the skins of children.

Twisting, whispering,
Scattering all the leaves everywhere.
Swirling in and out of the houses
Banging on the doors
Then it *stops!*
Silence all around.

Siobhan McAulay (11)
Painsley Catholic High School

THE MILLENNIUM

A new year's started, it's not the end.
The millennium's here, more to come
pack your bags, tell your mum
get out of town and have some fun.
A trip to the Dome would do no harm
or the big wheel, sit and be calm.
Tell your mum it will be alright
just relax and have some fun in town.
Don't be a bore, celebrate the millennium in style.

Clare Beech (13)
Painsley Catholic High School

PETS

I've just had an idea
I think I would like a pet
But really I'm puzzled
On which pet to choose
There's rabbits, fish, lizards and dogs
There's snakes, spiders, hamsters and frogs
There's guinea pigs, gerbils, chipmunks and cats
There's horses, ponies, birds and bats
Snakes slither along, silently hissing
Rabbits run around their run
Splat, whoops I trod on a spider
Whoosh, wow that bat's really a glider
But after this I'm not really sure
If I am interested in a pet anymore.

Joanne Parry (11)
Painsley Catholic High School

DRAGON

Kicking off the ground and into the air,
I feel the wind rush through my hair.
Turning my broomstick I see my sight,
A jet-black dragon rushing through the night.
With a pulse of speed the target is nearer,
I can get it now, the image is clearer.
Lurching forward I make a snatch,
I won't let go, I'm firmly attached.
The dragon bears a face of fury,
I'm feeling tense, I start to worry.
A flash of light and a surge of heat,
Its fiery breath I cannot defeat.

Anthony Callan (14)
Painsley Catholic High School

SCHOOL - THE RETURN

I got up bright and early on one school day,
I had my breakfast and then it struck me, we no longer had Mrs Kay!
While dashing for the bus I began to dread,
Why do we have to have Briggs, I'm sure he'll have my head.

I arrived at school soaked and late,
First day back with Briggs, oh I can't wait!
Dashing to form was a bit of a struggle,
As I kept slipping in many a puddle.

Form was over very quick,
Briggs is next, I think I feel sick.
Sir! Sir! I don't feel too well.
A long silence then the voice from hell!

'Well the medical room is stuffy, you'd be better in here son!'
They always say that, I just want to get away from him,
'Please can I go Sir, come on?'
'Well if you put it like that, *no* ' he replied,
I took a deep breath then sighed.

Well break came at last but he let us out late.
We didn't get much time, which wasn't too great.
Our class slowly began to march upstairs,
We entered the room and returned to our chairs.

The next lesson was too boring to explain,
We then went to dinner, which was very plain.
Then the return to room 9,
Where we knew things were not going to be fine!

When at last the lesson was done,
We were late out so I had to run,
Back to the bus, back to safety,
Thank goodness I was going home, didn't think I'd survive that day!

I woke up the next day and thought eh?
That wasn't a nightmare, it did happen yesterday!

Steven Luke (13)
Painsley Catholic High School

MY DIALECT POEM FOR NATIONAL POETRY DAY

I'm sitting ere, a poem I am writin,
My pencil I'm chewin and a bitin.
The words I cannot find, the rhythm not excitin,
But it's better than goin out fightin.

My friends want me to be one of the lads,
I'm tryin hard to keep up with the latest fads.
Hangin out down the park is really cool,
Listenin to music is what we do as a rule.

Discussin how to chat up girls,
Whether to choose brunette or blonde with curls.
We talk about computer games and
Fast cars we would like to drive,
Dreams or reality, depends how hard we strive.

I want to make a difference with my life,
In time I'd like to be a husband and marry me a wife.
Settle down have kids, holidays in the sun
And be the apple of someone's eye then have a lot of fun.

Simon Weston (12)
Painsley Catholic High School

LIFE

She speaks and they listen, but fail to hear her cries,
She weeps her pain, but her words they do not realise,
She questions her own truth, but how greatly they ignore,
She craves for answers, but her questions they do not understand.

They proclaim a truth so wrong and so false, a whisper she speaks
but is now denied,
They look so hard for something to see, a light she finds but there is
no longer a flame,
They promise the truth but change seems too unjust, a power she feels
but again is repressed,
They find a way forward to follow and inspire, she stands alone
but too helpless to see.

Her face so scarred by deep emotions, her dreams she longs to express,
Her eyes cannot cry true pain, her words cannot perceive,
Her image she can no longer convey, her life she cannot change,
Her truth she will never rebuild, her hope now lies shattered and gone.

Rachel Nixon (15)
Painsley Catholic High School

MY BOX

I have a box, full of thoughts and memories
Inside this box:
Are my thoughts and memories which flow like an everlasting waterfall
of anxiety
My imagination drifts free, flying like a butterfly
It's like a database of my life
Clasped in an everlasting memory.
There are photos, images and illusions of my deepest fantasy.
This is Heaven to me.

Tawny Hill (12)
Painsley Catholic High School

HORRID LAND

In this very horrid land,
where my feet go numb while I stand,
The mud covers my feelings and hurt inside,
like my loved ones smiling lovingly in my mind,
For if I don't return for tea just by chance,
arriving late from flea-ridden country called France,
Do not stand by my grave and start to stare,
I am not a dead man, I do not belong there,
For I am the crow calling and the snowflakes falling,
and I am the man calling and giving the gas warning,
The bodies of my friends litter the ground,
they lie there not making a sound,
Then I pray if only the King could have seen what I have seen,
this war would never have been.
In this very horrid land.

Simon Carnwell (14)
Painsley Catholic High School

RUGBY

Racing madly forwards like wild animals,
The lion-hearted player,
Collides with the rampaging rhino,
The elephant jumps aside
And he shakes the earth,
He's afraid of a small mouse in sneakers,
The score is thirty-five all . . .
Second-half of the creature feature,
The mouse is sent off the pitch,
The lion's team is sure to win,
It's every animal for himself!

Lauretta Fernando-Smith (13)
Painsley Catholic High School

THE BOY NEXT DOOR

The boy next door is oh so fine
How I wish he could be mine
With short black hair and manly build
He's the fittest bloke in all the world.

He's tall and smooth and really slick
With his Pi x 5 and his metre stick
I've always liked the clever type
To set my pulses racing
Get caught up in the girlish type
The noises I am making
When I see this fella stride along
How I wish he could be mine
Maybe I should write a song . . .
Hold on . . .

He's 29!

Lucy Harvey (13)
Painsley Catholic High School

PETROL

The petrol price is high.
The petrol price is low.
No one wants to know.
If the petrol goes down, will Blair go?
It's always on the telly.
The protesters say he's smelly.
I wouldn't pay high price petrol
I'd try my best to get it low,
So out in the car I could go.

Gregory Cashmore (12)
Painsley Catholic High School

COMPUTERS

Computers are a nightmare,
Full of crazy things,
Some say they're the future,
But I hate what the future brings!
You'll be sitting there for hours
Waiting for the programme to shut,
Oh yes you guessed it . . . another power cut!
You load back up the computer,
There's errors on the screen,
You're screaming at the monitor,
Please don't be mean!
There's sweat on your forehead,
Your fist is getting tighter,
I wish I had a petrol bomb and a cigarette lighter!

Dean Phillips (13)
Painsley Catholic High School

LIFE

We take it for granted
As it whizzes by
Not really using it carefully
It's a precious thing
But no one knows why
Then it's gone in a flash
From before your eyes
And you understand how
Treasured it is
When you've lost it all
It was yours and his.

Katie Burgess (14)
Painsley Catholic High School

VOICES

Persecution, oppression, abuse, discrimination
The voices of those call out in terror.
The voices of the oppressors call out scornfully.
Why, I can't understand, for those who persecute cannot possibly
Gain pleasure from abusing those who differ.

The voices of the victims, their lives oppressed by persecutors.
Why do they differ?
They may look, or sound different, but their souls remain the same
As any other human being.
Lives tainted by insults,
Souls sodden with tears.

We look at a soul, she sits in her room,
In the darkness.
Her tears merge into the red blood that seeps from her wrists,
Her arms are scarred.
Her mind is tortured by evil words.
Her life is ending, but why?
An evil word, a call of abuse.

Their voices cry out in terror,
But does anybody hear them?

Laura Brown (16)
Painsley Catholic High School

THE SEA

To feel the warm breeze on my face
Is some kind of sweet embrace.
To watch the stars twinkle in the sky,
If I had the choice forever there I would lie.

This is my Heaven for that I am sure
I want to stay here forever more.
The moon is in and not a person in sight.
The sea is vicious when it is night
Tomorrow once more,
I will watch the shore.

Laura Ryan (11)
Painsley Catholic High School

NANA

Nana used to squash blackberries to make blackberry sauce,
She'd do it so fine.
Squash, squash on the breadboard,
She'd end up with a sort of delicious red mud.

And she'd peel and core Bramleys for apple pie.
Sometimes I'd trim the pastry,
Trim, trim, with a bright knife.
Then I'd edge it round with a neat fork so it used to look like a small
bird had been walking round the rim.

Then she'd stir the custard,
Thicker and thicker it became.
Grandad Jack would then come in smiling from the garden.
It was a nice, slow Sunday - the blackbird would wag its Sunday-best
tail.
Then Nana, Grandad and I would all tuck in around the kitchen table.

We will miss the blackberry pies, the Yorkshire puddings, the steak and
kidney pies,
But most of all Nana we will miss you.

Emily Birks (15)
Painsley Catholic High School

MY WONDERFUL WORLD

My wonderful world would be,
Golden sands with the splish slash of the blue sea.
The sand would be like a nice fresh ice-cream.

My wonderful world would be,
Blue skies with the sun beaming down.
The blue skies would remind me
Of those days at home in the summer holidays.

My wonderful world would be,
Going on a holiday somewhere hot
With deserted beaches and the fresh coast breeze blowing.
Seeing children playing on the crisp yellow sand.

My wonderful world would be,
Green grass with brightly coloured flowers growing into
The garden,
The flowers would be like the ones at St James' palace.

My wonderful world would be,
Where there are no war, no debt and treat
Everybody fairly.
This would be my wonderful world.

Robert Holloway (12)
Painsley Catholic High School

DOLPHINS

Dolphins are gentle and kind,
And they have a very clever mind.
Swimming with their family, far out at sea.
How I wish they would swim with me.

When the sun is going down and the moon going up.
The dolphins jump and play.
Every day is the same,
Jumping, playing and catching prey.

We try to get a glimpse of them standing on the shore,
Waiting for the moment they come out to play some more.
But we must never forget that these beautiful creatures are wild.
And we must try to look after them so they will survive.

There are many kinds of dolphins,
Different sizes, different shapes.
Many end up in fishing nets,
Trying to escape.

So when you are out shopping,
Remember them at play.
And buy the things that say 'dolphin friendly'
And that will make my day.

Louise Hanly (13)
Painsley Catholic High School

ABOUT AN INCOMPETENT THIEF

Dave the thief is the best in town,
With his stealing skills he'll sneak around,
As he climbs the wall, inch by inch,
He begins to ponder what to pinch,
He smashes through a window with an almighty thudd!
And trapezes around leaving footprints of mud,
He'll grab anything but won't hang around,
As the shrieking alarm begins to sound.
He panicks and leaps through the window he smashed,
Falling to the ground, about to be mashed!
Thirty, twenty, ten metres away,
For all his crimes, he's about to pay!
But look! Here comes a garbage truck
Dave'll be saved! Of good! What luck,
The truck comes closer, nearer to Dave,
Will he survive? It'll be a close shave!
Oh no, Oh God! The truck drove by . . .
Splat the pavement's just been crowned,
Dave's body now lying there flat on the ground,
Dave was a thief, small and fat,
Now he's been splattered and eaten by rats,
The pancake is headed straight to his grave
For this is the end of the great thief Dave.

Michael Sleath (13)
Painsley Catholic High School

MY ONLY UNCLE

He was my only uncle,
But he soon went away,
He would take me to the races,
Spoil me for the day,
He would buy chocolate and sweets just for me,
He was the kind, gentle giant for all to see.

He was my only uncle
But now he's gone away
I hate the people who used him and think he's faded away,
But he's up there watching down on us every single day.

He was my only uncle, but now he's gone away!

Ruth Powell (13)
Painsley Catholic High School

PAINTBALL!

With the gun in my hand I feel invincible
I only wish that I was invisible
Ducking, diving, hiding behind trees
Holding in the pain as my hands begin to freeze.
Scan the area to see if it's clear
Plucking up the courage, I'm really near
Step out of the bush, not a sound
There has got to be someone around
Running stealthily, I can see the flag
Then all of a sudden I see two gigantic paintballs
                            heading towards me!
Bang! Bang! Right between the eyes!
Thank God for the face protector!
Virtually blind but still running
Why can I still hear paintballs coming?
Only ten metres away from the flag
When this is all over I'll be glad.
I grab hold of the flag in my hands
Victory!
Bang! Bang!
Aaaaahhhhh!
Game over!

Anthony Withington (15)
Painsley Catholic High School

WHAT HAPPENED TO HER? - WHY DID SHE CHANGE?

What's happened to her?
Why did she change?

She used to care about us
Now all she cares about is popularity
Popularity, what does it mean
That you love yourself or that someone else loves you.

What's happened to her?
Why did she change?

Fake mates or real mates,
You'd think it was an easy choice
Than why did she choose fake?

What's happened to her?
Why did she change?

I miss her so much
Why doesn't she come back?
No one else cares
All they do is slag her off.

What's happened to her?
Why did she change?

Her new mates are horrible
They are only out for themselves
They go out with anyone and everyone
Why does she like them?

What's happened to her?
Why did she change?

She turned into one of them
Going out with loads of lads
Accidentally on purpose forgetting homework.

What happened to her?
Why did she change?

I can't believe she said those things,
Especially after I stuck up for her
She doesn't deserve us
She belongs as one of them
She was so horrible I hate her.

What's happened to her?
Why did she change?

If I hate her why do I still miss her so much?

Claudia Porteous (13)
Painsley Catholic High School

PEACEFULLY GLIDING

My rosy red cheeks are all you can see,
From sweeping winds dashing across the snow,
Barely being able to see my hands,
Wrapped up warm in layers of attire,
I navigate swiftly, silently, smoothly on my skies,
Up and down always a surprise,
Never stuttered though never stammered.
Placidly swaying like I could fly.
No scenery to be seen, no people to spot,
Cause snow that descends onto the unfriendly grounds,
Peacefully gliding.

Sarah Dick (15)
Painsley Catholic High School

MY SISTER

On her face is always a smile,
I can tell it from a mile.
Her big brown eyes that I can see,
Sometimes tell a lie to me.

The day she nearly passed away,
I'll never forget that horrible day.
The scars, they will always remain,
But fortunately she feels no pain.

She's always there when I feel down,
Her smile will take my worried frown.
When she's there I feel so glad,
But when she's not I feel so sad.

We sometimes fight,
But only because I'm right,
Her craze for driving,
She thinks it's exciting.

We're a pair together,
Forever and ever.

Nicola Borthwick (14)
Painsley Catholic High School

WINTER

Soft white crumbly flakes of snow,
Drifted quietly onto the ground below.
Children are laughing, playing,
Christmas songs old people are saying,
The sky a ray of shimmering blue.
Complete with birds and fluffy clouds too.
Then came a shadow dominating all,
From a fierce shadow, standing proud and tall.

The frosted windows sparkled in the light,
Thousands of fairy lights, each one bright.
Decorated the dark mysterious Christmas tree,
A present for Sarah and one for Lee.
Lay under the Christmas tree that night
They were all packed in very tight.
In the morning the children came,
For a present with this name,
Until this day,
Next year children will play.

Sara Lander (14)
Painsley Catholic High School

HALF A GLANCE (DEEP DOWN INSIDE)

Look inside, take a glance,
The outside still there, shining through
And yet being blocked by the transparent shadows.
The immaculate evil, trust of deception is seen,
In half a glance of a blurred, perfect vision,
See what's there, look back and it's not,
Like a predator watching its prey, its life,
A life will flash by, bye,
Look inside, take a glance,
The normal wonders you will find
So easy and yet impossible,
A burning inside you, alight with a flame so cold,
No deeper could you go,
And yet, shallower by far,
So many of the lightest shadows you'll find
In the place you'd least expect: deep down inside.

Joseph Wheatley (14)
Painsley Catholic High School

NIGHTMARES

Nightmares are funny things,
You wake up with a sweat,
As the evening draws in you know it's time for bed,
Come on now darling, go on get into bed,
Then you drift asleep and there you
Know horrific things will make the hairs
Stand on your head,
It seems so real,
But you know it's not,
From monsters in your bed to horrific
Things in your head,
As dawn nears,
Your fears start to grow,
As you know you may not finish
The amazing dream which is in tow,
As you must get out of bed,
It plays on your mind all day long
And as evening dawns, you can't wait
To go to bed to finish that terrifying
Dream, which is still stuck in your head!

Ann Bailey (13)
Painsley Catholic High School

BOYS

Boys,
Small tall,
Some small,
Some ugly,
Others gorgeous
Fat, thin, whatever they may be,
Someone, somewhere at one point will fancy them
At that point in time,
They will adore themselves.

Boys,
Some thin,
Some fat,
Some hard,
Some weak,
Some with a six pack and muscles,
Others with thin skiny arms,
Boys, boys, boys.

Sally Wrightson (13)
Painsley Catholic High School

SCHOOL

School has come yet again
And oh how it is a pain.
Get your pens and pencils out,
This is what the teachers shout,
Next it's on to maths,
Where there'll be no laughs,
Why does it have to be so dull?
The class is a quiet lull,
Maths has passed,
It's break at last,
The whistle blows,
The pupils moan,
Now it's PE,
With Mrs O'Neill,
Then it's RE, with Miss Meek,
I have her 3 times a week,
Science is next,
We'll have to write loads of text,
At last the final bell rings.

Alison Hewitt (14)
Painsley Catholic High School

THE OLYMPICS

The Olympic Games are now well on the way,
Great Britain's hopes, well what can we say.
The atheletes dream of a medal chance,
With swimmers style and gymnast dance.
The atheletes run with tremendous speed,
We need to get them into the lead.
The heats are over the final's begun,
So come on GB, run, run, run.
Hockey, atheletes teams galore,
The sports are being played more and more.
Now we'll have to wait another four years,
The atheletes dreams may become fears,
So come on GB what's left to say
We can win next time another day.

Sarah Lamburn (13)
Painsley Catholic High School

BEHIND THE OLD STONE WALLS!

The secret garden lies behind
The wall of stone that acts as a blind,
No one's been in there for a hundred years,
Since the time when parents were called Madams and Sirs.
No one but the robin has seen the beauty,
Or the gardener ghost who still does his duty.
There are rumours and rhymes of what happened in those times,
But we still don't know which one is true,
So we wait for the young boy or girl, to find the golden clue.

Anna Dougherty (13)
Painsley Catholic High School

THOUGHTS

They cause problems which need to be solved
Those of which go untold.

They jumble up inside your head,
Which tumble out when in hate.

They can be good, they can be bad,
They could mean, evil, treachery or something sad.

Often miscellaneous thoughts run wild through my head,
Causing hopelessness and despair.

Thoughts can mean trouble and affliction.

Weary minds worry and hate,
However, sometimes bringing goodness or even fate.

Jennifer Sladek (14)
Painsley Catholic High School

TV FREAK

My friend Bob is a TV freak,
He watches it 7 days a week,
He says that he gets his exercise
By pressing the buttons with his thighs,
The numbers on the buttons have been worn away,
He is on the couch every day
That is Bob the TV freak,
People mistake him for a geek.

James Bickerton (13)
Painsley Catholic High School

BATTLE SCARS

Colours flashed before my eyes,
It was now or never,
Do or die,
Then and now, now and then,
May never such a battle occur again.

Tears streamed down my face,
The bloody field which I embraced.
The stench of death lingered in the air,
Dying men, lying in despair.

On the battlefield, two sides have clashed,
The ground lined with bodies mashed.
Was all this death worth all the cost?
Whether we had won or lost.

Phillip Shaughnessy (14)
Painsley Catholic High School

THE WATER CYCLE

I am at the top of the mountains,
As high as the clouds,
But soon I come running down as fast
As a cheetah.
I join a river rushing like a herd,
I plop into the sea like a heavy raindrop.
I start to rise like a kite in the wind,
Suddenly I form something nearly as
Thick as fairy liquid.
Soon I come falling down as fast
As a sky glider,
To my amazement I'm back where I was
Ready to go again.

Elizabeth Barry (11)
Painsley Catholic High School

THE RACE

The horses wait on the line
Tension is in the air all around
The gun blasts to signal the start
They gallop off down the course
Pounding their hooves firm on the ground
Elegantly showing their power
To the jockeys it is all a blur
Everything rushes past in a second
Winning is everything
Losing is nothing
The finish draws closer
Everything happens at once
The jockey looks behind him
To see the others cross the line
Now he's champion.

Craig Forrester (13)
Painsley Catholic High School

NIGHT

I looked out of my window,
The sky was filled with darkness.
Stars were hidden by clouds,
Frost was glistening on the grass.
Eerie shadows stretched over the garden,
It is now nearly midnight and almost pitch-black,
A very dim light is glowing from the moon.
Everywhere is still and silent.

Luke Shaughnessy (12)
Painsley Catholic High School

THE SKY

Blue as the ocean
Quiet with no motion,
Swift as a bird,
Never to be heard.
Still as a rock,
Like the sea beside the dock,
Whistling like a flute,
You overhear it with the mute.

Happy as a playful girl,
Fragile as a precious pearl,
Sweet as a cherry drop,
Until the clouds suddenly pop!

Sharp as a knife
Blue sky reaching for its life,
Noisy as a hyena,
The dark sky getting meaner,
Grumpy as an old man,
Who's been hit with a frying pan.

Hannah Richardson (11)
Painsley Catholic High School

CHILDREN

They scream when you tell them no,
They throw tantrums in the shops,
They always take Nanny's side,
Because Nanny always knows best.

They colour on your wallpaper,
They spill drinks all over the floor,
They cost you a fortune at Christmas,
And still ask for more.

When it comes to parties,
Do you really need to ask?
Jelly and ice-cream are the words,
And the exhausting task.

Above all of this,
Your child is still the best,
It wrote its name before your friends,
And came top, above all the rest.

Nicole Rawle (14)
Painsley Catholic High School

POEM

Not knowing what to write,
Not an idea in sight,
A total mental block
My head's going for the chop,
A pen dragging over paper,
Not writing anything special
Just a little message
So I will not get in trouble
I have to write a poem see,
On whatever we want it to be.
This poem is really poor
My brains are spread over the floor
I know I'm not a clever girl
My head is getting into a whirl,
I've never been a poet
And I honestly do know it.
I'll try and do a brainstorm
A plan or something like that
I'll write my poem quickly
Then I think I'll have a chat.

Vicky Lund (14)
Painsley Catholic High School

MY FOOTIE MATCH

I woke up this morning
And said to me mum,
Hey up! What's up,
I need to feed my tum.

She made me some brekkie,
T'was a full English one,
It has sausages and beans,
With chips in a bun.

I went to training
Had a game later on,
We needed to win by
Three goals to none.

We practiced our shooting
And tackling too,
We needed to pass
To get our way through.

After training,
I went to Mackie D's,
I spilt tomato ketchup
And it landed on my knees.

When I got home
I got my kit and
Washed my golden boots
To make them spick and span.

During the game
We went 1-0 up
And at half-time,
We had a drink of 7-Up.

We carried on the game,
Then scored our second goal,
The match was nearly over
And we needed Andy Cole.

We went surging forward
We got in a shot,
The keeper knocked it over,
So we thought we had it lost.

We whipped in the corner
The keeper punched it clear,
I smacked the ball back in
And it went very near . . .

'Goal!'

The ball went in the net
And then the whistle went,
The game was finally over,
Yes! Time to celebrate!

We had won the footie league
And the footie cup.
Everyone congratulated me,
I said, 'Yo, thank you very much.'

When I finally got home,
After all the fun,
I told the score line to,
My father and my mum.

Michael Gamble (12)
Painsley Catholic High School

DEAD

I lay, numb from the terror ricocheting off my body
As my unbelieving eyes witnessed yet another massacre
Bloodshed, screams from the innocent audience
Bullets flying through the once peaceful world.

Bombs landed obliterating all in their path
An accumulation of broken lives lay scattered before me
Consumed by terror and devastation
Childrens' cries echoed through my empty mind.

Explosions encirling me, entwined with desperate whimpers
A world once passive turned into one of evil and brutality
Soldiers unfeeling took guard, taking no pity on even the young
I broke down, let out my whimper, the only strength I still had.

I crawled, pulling my limp body over broken remains
Blood streaming from the hole ripped in my arm
Fear enveloped me, crushing what little hope my mind contained
Frozen, still, shaking from the possibilities that lay uncovered.

One last desperate attempt at survival
Legs pushing under me, eager to get away
It hit me, ripping my weakened chest open
My legs came from under me as I hit the ground
Dead.

Amy Rhodes (16)
Painsley Catholic High School

COME ON PONY LET'S GALLOP AWAY

Come on pony, let's gallop away,
People to see, in only one day,
We've got to hurry,
They'll be in a flurry,
Come on pony, let's go, okay?

Come on pony, let's start on our route,
There will be people who shout and cars that will toot,
They do not like us,
Not even the bikers,
Come on pony, let's start on our route.

Come on pony, let's fly to the moon,
It won't take much time, we'll be there real soon,
We'll see all the stars,
See Venus or Mars,
Come on pony, let's fly to the moon.

Come on pony, it's time to go home,
I know it's not fair, but there's no need to moan,
There's no need for weeping,
We soon will be sweeping,
Up to the fields that you love to roam.

Louise Beardmore (13)
Painsley Catholic High School

I FEEL

There is fame enough for the hero,
who dwells on his height of fame,
I feel for the disappointed,
for those who missed their aim.

I feel for the breathless runner,
the eager, anxious soul,
who falls with his strength exhausted,
almost in sight of the goal.

I feel for the hearts that break in silence,
with a sorrow all unknown,
for those who need companions,
yet walk their ways alone.

Yet deep inside I know and feel,
that somewhere out in space,
there is a prize for that spent runner,
who barely lost the race.

For the plan would be imperfect,
unless it held some sphere,
that paid for the toil and talent,
and love that are wasted here.

Adrian Long (13)
Painsley Catholic High School

OUR DAY OUT

We went to a roadside shop,
There we stole half of the sweets,
Then we went to the zoo,
Saw the parrots trying to talk.

Next to the spooky castle,
Pile of crumbling old bricks,
The beach was our next stop,
There we had a game of football.

While we were playing football,
Mrs Kay noticed Carol had gone,
She had gone to the cliffs,
Briggs found her and brought her back.

Rock 'n roll music at the fairground,
Waltzers, big wheel and darts,
Cowboy Briggs ate candyfloss,
And won a goldfish for Carol.

The kids pile on the coach,
Back to school they go,
Briggs ruins the film that shows,
The day he's had fun.

James Truswell (14)
Painsley Catholic High School

OH HOW I WISH I HAD A PUPPY

Oh how I wish I had a puppy,
I would give her loads of treats,
I would make her heel and kneel
And I'd give her loads of meat.

We would roam around the footie pitch,
Playing loads of catch,
It would just be me and my bitch,
We would be so very attached.

Oh how I wish I had a puppy,
I would build her a fantastic kennel,
I'll throw her the ball, all day long
And she'll lick me with her tongue.

I'll take her for walks every day,
Not forgetting Sundays,
She'll be the best at dog shows,
Which takes place on Mondays.

So why can't I have a puppy,
To be my best companion.

Sarah Atkin (13)
Painsley Catholic High School

HOMELESS AND DYING

Cold and hungry on the street,
Watching people as they eat,
Wrapped in my blanket of despair,
They don't look, they don't care.

Now the night is closing in,
A broken arm and a bruised shin,
Alone and scared I wait for the end,
Upon no one I can now depend.

Bloodstained clothes, wet and worn,
I lie in wait of the approaching dawn,
My heart and soul are filled with fear,
Because I know the time is here.

My tired eyes begin to close,
The rain and snow are now my foes,
The ground around me turns to red,
I remain silent until I'm dead.

Alison Bailey (15)
Painsley Catholic High School

HOPE

Though your heart may ache a while,
Though your face may lose its smile,
Though there may seem no way out,
You've got to stay hopeful, never doubt.

Though your life is torn to shreds,
Though the world may seem worthless,
Though you're finding it hard to cope,
Chin up, smile, there's always hope.

For as there's sunshine after rain,
Gladness often follows pain,
Though your journey may seem long
You can be hopeful, you can stay strong.

The tears you cry can be wiped away,
You will find happiness some day,
Believe in yourself, you can cope and
Whatever happens, there's always hope.

Laura Barnes (14)
Painsley Catholic High School

UNUSUAL, DIFFERENT AND NEW

Depending who you're speaking to,
Dialect can at times be funny.
You might hear 'Hiya Mate!'
Or 'How are ya honey?'

If you were to travel around the UK,
You'd learn an unusual word every day.

Will ya be called love, sweetheart or darling?
Depends really where you're living.
Duck, pet or dear.
To me all sound odd and queer.

If you were to travel around the UK,
You'd learn a different word every day.

Feeling hungry? Time for tea!
Fancy a bap, a bun, or even a butty?
Perhaps a roll, a cob,
Or just a good old sarny?

If you were to travel around the UK,
You'd learn a new word every day.

Bradley Ford (12)
Painsley Catholic High School

ARMAGEDDON

In the year 2002
A big comet shall hit me and you
Anarchy will rule the nation
Out with law in with dictation.

Guns and fire
People's desire
Fear eruption
Mass distruction.

The world is a blaze,
With a thick black haze,
Terror is unleashed
This is the end of peace.

Now the world's defence has failed
Death and evil has prevailed
Now the Earth has reached its doom
Welcome to Hell, see you soon.

Sam Dougherty (15)
Painsley Catholic High School

FORMULA ONE FAILURES

As I put back on my leathers,
Grab my helmet by its teather,
Wondering whether I will win,
Or wind up trashed, in the bin.

It is qualifying time, right now,
My chance to prove myself,
Pole position could be mine,
Or qualify last for the twelfth time.

I'm in the race at twenty-first,
Just one place from the back.
At least I'm running in the race,
Oh my God! Whack!

Well now I'm out of the race,
My car in many parts,
There's no glory for this driver,
Just a lot of broken hearts.

Kieran Timms (13)
Painsley Catholic High School

THE RACE

The fans were cheering for their man,
The race was nearly on,
The starter says, 'Get set' and then he bangs the gun.

A good start was needed, as the crowd was nervous too,
Everyone stormed off the line and out the blocks I flew,
The race was there for the taking matching stride by stride,
In the first hundred meters, I couldn't get past them no matter
How hard I tried.

My thoughts were on the starter as he banged the gun,
People started to come past me and now the pursuit was on,
I made a dash from the pack as I came round the bend,
I was there with the others up front and now I could see the end.

The race was on and I was second with one man in my sight,
The lad was tall, fast and smooth as I watched him in mid flight,
I started to gain speed as we approached the line,
Then I cruised past the rival and I knew the race was mine.

Ryan Bettaney (13)
Painsley Catholic High School

THE GOLDEN YEARS

So they say, life begins at forty,
But I don't care about all of that!
My life began all of last year,
By completely annoying SATs.

'You'll grow up one day, be mature,
With a wife and kids,'
But don't give a damn
I'll be an invalid!

'You will take many hard exams,
You better get a good mark!'
But I just wanna stay, young,
Just playin' in the park!

That's right, I don't wanna grow old,
Just be at the legal age!
Loads of girls and alcohol
Collecting minimum wage!

Matthew Goodall (14)
Painsley Catholic High School

MIN

You'll never find a cat as dozy as Min.
Even though she's lovable, she is so very dim,
She thinks that she's a lion as she prowls around the yard,
Assuming that she'll catch something if she sits still keeping guard.

Her tongue hangs out and her ear is curled,
She always seems to be in another world,
There's absolutely nothing dainty about Min,
She plods around heavy footed and loves to sleep in the bin.

I don't think she can see much as her eyes are so crossed,
She charges round like she owns the place - as if she's the boss,
She loves to tease the dog by playing with his tail,
For Min, life is nothing but a game.

Despite the fact that Min is so muddled,
She always wants a loving cuddle,
When her hard days work is done, catching mice and having fun,
She curls up by the fire and dreams of days to come!

Elizabeth Dale (14)
Painsley Catholic High School

THE WALL

You
    Sit
        There
             And
                Stare
                    At
                        Me
                    Homework
              Settled
        Upon
    Your
Knee.
    Your
        Eyes
            Glare
                For
                    Inspiration
                Screaming
        Out
    In
Desperation.

        'I can't do this, it's such a bore!'
Well
    I
Can't
    Help
I'm
    Just
A
    Wall.

Lisa Taylor (14)
Painsley Catholic High School

IF I HAD A . . .

If I had a wishing well
I think I'd have to ask
That I could have some happiness
I don't care if it would pass
A single moment of pure bliss
A lovers sweet and tender kiss,
A smile across a stranger's face
An instance of God's delicate grace.

If I had a wishing well
I think I'd have to ask
That I could find my one true love
Heaven sent from up above
My darling angel pure of heart
From him I could never, ever part,
Sweet saviour of my eternal soul
His love would engulf me whole
In return I'd give my life
If he would take me as his wife.

If I had a wishing well
I think I'd have to ask
That I could find some beauty
Or else get a better mask.

Laura Cooper (14)
Painsley Catholic High School

CHRISTMASTIME IS DRAWING NEAR

Stockings hanging by the fire,
The Christmas tree in the room to admire.
The sound of Christmas carols sung once again
And visions of elves as queer little men.
Rudolph with his red glowing nose
And is Santa real? Well nobody knows.
Presents sitting under the tree,
Waiting there for you and me.
Sledges and sleighs tumble down the hills
And Christmas decorations laid out on all window sills.
Christmas is getting near
And before you can blink,
It's arrived and it's here.

Laura Gilbert (12)
St Thomas More Catholic College

SNOWFLAKES

S oft snow coming down
N ever to go up again.
O ver the world it falls every
W inter.
F alling like little stars
L ovely white shiny cold flakes.
A t winter there is snow on the roads.
K icking and screaming not wanting to melt.
E ven when it begins to thaw you can make
S nowmen and snowballs.

John Batista (12)
St Thomas More Catholic College

THE WONDERS OF THE WOOD

Trees, smell the bark,
Crowded branches,
Evil monsters,
The glistening moonlit sky surrounded by dark.
A ragged wilderness bare of habitations,
Confined with tall trees,
Beware you nations.
Engraved footprints of weird strangers,
Stalkers, hunters, eager for their prey,
Travelling by unaware of the dangers.
The beautiful owls are angels,
Their eyes glisten,
Whilst bats are devils,
Their shivering screech - *listen!*

Natalie Kelsall
St Thomas More Catholic College

IMAGINATION

I can fly across the sky,
With my wings spread out wide.
I can wake up on Mars,
I can drive flying cars.
In my world food is free,
All the people dance with glee.
Children singing to hip-hop,
Teenage boys play some rock.
My world is Planet Fun,
There'll be no nagging from your mum.

Hayley Johnson (12)
St Thomas More Catholic College

MY POEM ABOUT MY KITTEN

Ears pricked up,
Wide awake.
My kitten is small and soft,
Its little eyes glaring wide
Strolling about with its pride
Running here, miaowing there
He does all this without a care
Give him string or a piece of cotton
It will jump and fall on his bottom
Till he gets his own way
Which is his favourite meal of the day
His fur is soft like silk,
His tail is precious like gold,
That little kitten of mine is very bold.

Emma Pugh (12)
St Thomas More Catholic College

A POEM ABOUT MY HAMSTER

My hamster playing in his wheel,
He only stops for his meals.

In his house he falls asleep,
He covers himself really deep.

Then when he nibbles at his cage,
I scream and shout with anger and rage.

I take him in my hand
His little body covered in sand.

Then when I clean him out,
He runs and runs and runs about.

Natalie Jade Goodwin (11)
St Thomas More Catholic College

DUSTY DUSTBIN

His name is Dusty,
He's a bin,
He's very smelly,
And really thin,
He's got a red nose,
And twinkle toes,
He is yellow,
And really mellow,
That's why he's my friend,
And he's got a great trend.

People treat him like an old bin
And think he's a lump of tin,
But he's not 'cause he's the best,
He's better than all the rest.

Laura Howe (13)
St Thomas More Catholic College

ANIMALS ALL AROUND

Animals in the jungle
Crashing through the trees,
Elephants splashing in the pool,
Monkeys herd to sneeze.

Tigers roaring as they hunt
Zebras drinking by the pool,
Leopards sitting in the trees,
Then came the rhinos
Trying to keep cool.

Siân Law (11)
St Thomas More Catholic College

POVERTY

The world today is full of greed,
Some people are living well,
There's lots of hunger in this world,
How much? No one can tell.

People homeless, starving, dying,
It really is quite sad,
There's nothing worse than poverty,
It really makes me mad.

Hot meals in front of us each day,
There's nothing more we need.
There's too much hunger in the world,
With starving mouths to feed.

Each day I wake, and wonder why,
People are blind to see,
There's no one doing anything
To end this poverty.

Jodie Stokes (11)
St Thomas More Catholic College

HOSPITAL

H   ospital is scary when you are hurt
O   ver the bedside people's veins burst
S   limy and sloppy, on goes the bandage
P   ensioners on the other side nicked my sandwich
I   n my bed I will lie still
T   rying to resist the red and black pill
A   ll the time I did it to look cool
L   ying to my mum to have the day off school.

Max Rochelle (12)
St Thomas More Catholic College

BADMINTON

A serve to the left
Return to the right
Lob over the top
Hurry on up, soon it is night

14-5, you're being thrashed
A few minutes later a set down
You're losing 1-0, you'd better come back
Or else you'll be out

Second set lost - you're out
Tears come, bat broken
Shake the man's hand
And disappear crying

Gets the silver medal
Still not pleased
But he'll be back to play him
Next year.

Matthew Wild (11)
St Thomas More Catholic College

MONSTERS

M ean monsters fat and green
O nly monsters can be this mean
N o one can stand this horrible sight
S ome of them can give you a tremendous fright
T en eyes they can have in their head
E ven 22 arms and legs so they can't fit in their bed
R eally ugly monsters can be
S limy, slippery like Mrs Slattery.

Daniel Bates (12)
St Thomas More Catholic College

POLTERGEIST

I heard a bang, Mum was out, I was all alone in my fear.
The clock was chiming, it struck midnight,
Outside it was dark, the moon shone bright,
The cat screeching, the dog was howling,
A crash downstairs startles me as I creak across the landing.

Worriedly, I go slowly down the stairs,
Into the kitchen but there's nothing there,
As I walk out and shut the door behind me.
A loud bang comes from the landing,
I go up and there's something there
And suddenly I hear things but there's nothing there.

Noises from upstairs, then from down,
I get confused as the moon frowns,
A light from beyond startles me,
It's shining through the window,
But then, I'm all in the dark.

Danielle Malvern (12)
St Thomas More Catholic College

HOMEWORK

H   orrid homework every day
O   ver and over
M   ad teachers giving it out
E   very day
W   orrying if it's right or wrong
O   ver and over, time and time again
R   ushing it for the next day
K   icking and screaming up to our rooms.

Richard Thompson (12)
St Thomas More Catholic College

BEYOND THE RAINBOW

Beyond the rainbow is a land,
With deep blue seas and pebbled sand.

The air is sweet from vibrant smells,
The flowers sing like ringing bells.

The people there drink out of silver shells,
As they dance around like tinkerbells.

No one cries everyone smiles,
They see their rainbow for miles and miles.

The waterfalls are like twinkling stars,
They shine and glisten from afar.

Is this the land of sugar skies
Where sugar fairies dance and smile?
        Or
Is it just my imagination running wild?

Laura Grundy (11)
St Thomas More Catholic College

A RAINBOW

A rainbow is streaks of colour
painted on a bright blue piece of paper.

A rainbow lights up the sky around us
with its beautiful colours.

A rainbow symbolises that the rain has gone
and it has taken its place in the sky.

A rainbow signals that it is a beautiful thing
that we could be if we tried.

Jake Bailey (11)
St Thomas More Catholic College

SPORTS

Sports are fun
We start at the gun.
We run really fast
And get there at last.

We run and run
Just for the fun.
We get there first
With a very bad thirst.

When someone gets hurt
We are alert.
It all goes well
Then goes the bell.

I feel like I'm dead
And I just want to go to bed.
Have a long night's sleep
And get up at the beep.

Sports are fun
We start at the gun.
We run really fast
And get there at last.

Natasha Taylor (12)
St Thomas More Catholic College

THE BOASTFUL GHOST

The boastful ghost flapped through a wall,
His white face full of glee,
'I'm much the bravest ghost there is,
A real ghoul,' said he.
'All living creatures, great and small,
Are terrified of me.'

Just then a bustling, bright-eyed mouse
Came hopping down the stair,
The ghost looked round, shrieked 'Help!'
And flew to tremble on a chair,
And, passing by, the tiny mouse,
Was heard to squeak 'Oh yeah?'

Ashley Mills (11)
St Thomas More Catholic College

FOOTBALL

Football, football
Is the best
We lose some matches
And win the rest.

Michael Owen
Alan Shearer
Get the ball
World Cup fever.

David Beckham
Gets the ball
Halftime comes
The score's 2 all.

Back on the pitch
It's now 3-2
And it's Alan Shearer
He's cut straight through.

Paul Scholes on the floor
He'd better get up or
We'll be out the door.

James Price (13)
St Thomas More Catholic College

BOOKS

Books are great,
Books are fun,
Books are here,
For everyone.

Poetry, adventure,
Romance too,
Different types of books
To suit you!

With a book
You can laugh and cry,
And mystery books
Leave you wondering why?

Books are great,
Books are fun,
Books are here,
For everyone.

Cheryl Clayton (11)
St Thomas More Catholic College

DOLPHINS

D iving through the water as fast as they can go
O ver the waves, under the waves, but not so slow
L ooking for food in the big wide sea
P laying with friends who want to be free
H eading with speed towards the beach
I   n less than a minute they will reach
N ever wants to touch the ground
S wimming in the sea is where they are found.

James Picariello (12)
St Thomas More Catholic College

CARS

Cars are cool
and really fast,
but only if
your licence lasts!

Orange cars,
red cars,
anything to
multicoloured cars.

Jazzy cars,
speedy cars,
ace cars,
weedy cars.

If I had a car,
it would have to be,
the fastest one
'cause it's just like me.

Matthew Tranah (12)
St Thomas More Catholic College

FISHING

F   ishing
I   s fun, especially when you use a
S   uperb whopping big
H   ook nothing can escape from
I   n my grasp the fish
N   ever
G   et away.

Paul Housley (13)
St Thomas More Catholic College

THE HAUNTED HOTEL

T here was a haunted house
H aunted it may be
E normous vampires live in the walls
   and they start scaring me

H uge witches walk around the floor
A monster sneaks out and strangles you
   by the door
U nhappy visitors demanding their money back
N asty creatures are in your bath
T he biggest spider crawling up your back
E very night hear fear in your mind
D evils stab you in the eye

H otel guests put onions in their room
   to keep vampires away from their rooms
O r keep the light on so they won't come at night
T hey can't bear to go in their room
   as it is not a lot of fun
E veryone is scared to bits
L iz the manager telling everyone to run.

Scott Smallman (12)
St Thomas More Catholic College

SAUSAGES

The silly soggy sausages
Sizzled softly spitting
In the seaside sun

Sally Shaw saw the
Sizzling sausages and
Started spitting like the sizzling sauce.

Matthew Watts (12)
St Thomas More Catholic College

MY HOUSEHOLD

Bang! My sisters door slams,
Boom! Boom! Goes her music upstairs,
Beep! Excuse her language,
My mum doesn't care.

The door bell chimes, ding, dong,
'You answer it' roared Dad from his chair,
The phone rings,
My mum doesn't care.

Steam hisses in the shower,
Water splashes everywhere,
Drip, drip, drip . . .
'It's trickling through the ceiling' squeals my sister,
My mum doesn't care.

Rachel Becker (11)
St Thomas More Catholic College

ROAD SAFETY

Stop! Look over here
Watch where you're going or else there might be some tears
Look both ways, don't be a dork
Look left and right before you start to walk.

Be safe, be happy
Don't worry, don't hurry
So if you want to live
Take this piece of advice I give
And do everything that I told you right
Even follow the safety code at night.

Rebecca Warren (12)
St Thomas More Catholic College

STOP BUGGING ME!

Why do you keep flying around that light
All day long and most of the night?

You really are annoying me now
I'm going to have to get you somehow.

Flying constantly in front of my eyes
I can't express how much I despise
The way you land up on my plate
Someday soon it will be too late.

I snap my hands up in the air
Trying to catch you unaware
I open my fist expecting to find
A little squashed body left behind.

But there you are up by the light
Dear oh dear what a terrible plight
As you fly into the blue light
Zap! What a relief, no more fly in sight.

Laura Pickard (11)
St Thomas More Catholic College

MONKEY JUNGLE

I was walking through the jungle
Where all I could see were the great big trees.
As I walked past the monkeys were screeching at me
I saw a great big one looking at me
He said 'I am the king, can't you see?
So get lost, ha, ha, hee.'
The monkeys ganged up and chased me away.

David Evans (12)
St Thomas More Catholic College

THE WRITER OF THIS POEM

The writer of this poem
is as funny as a clown,
as fast as the Internet
and never shows she's down.

The writer of this poem
is as tall as a tree,
as clever as a computer,
as friendly as you and me.

The writer of this poem
is as thin as a rake,
as cute as a hamster,
as slippery as a snake.

The writer of this poem
never ceases to amaze,
she's one in a million zillion,
or so the poem says.

Melissa Tideswell (11)
St Thomas More Catholic College

FOOTBALL

F ootball is fun,
O nly in the sun,
O h how I missed the goal,
T hat means I'll be on the dole,
B ut to the rescue,
A s the final whistle goes,
L ook out here comes extra time,
L et's hope that the ball is mine.

Daniel Hasdell (12)
St Thomas More Catholic College

THE MOON

The moon is a sparkling diamond,
It reminds me of a ring,
The moon has lots of humps and bumps,
But it's a wonderful thing.

The moon is an evil eye,
It watches all the time
The moon has a big bright light
Can you survive the fright?

The moon has a big round face
But it could never race
The moon has big googlie eyes
They look like cherry pies.

Phillip Tatton (11)
St Thomas More Catholic College

STORM WATCH

S   nowing, sleeting all day long
T   orrential rain flooding the rivers
O   ld folk getting scared
R   ivers bursting their banks
M   ajor earthquakes.

W   ater running down the street
A   nnoyed people
T   rying to save their homes
C   atching pets as they swim on by
H   oping that it will all die down.

Mark Boyles (12)
St Thomas More Catholic College

GHOST!

Creak! went the floorboards
as I entered the haunted house.

Suddenly I heard a strange noise
Bang! Bang! Bang!

I stepped outside quickly
with the wind whistling around me.

Smash! went the windows
I turned around quickly

And saw
>> *The ghost!*

David Bryan (12)
St Thomas More Catholic College

SPACE

Space is big, weird and free,
You can float with lots of glee.
Looking down upon the Earth,
Mercury, Mars, they came first.
As shooting stars shoot on by,
In the dark, starlit sky.

How I wish I could be
Up so high with the world to see.
Spaceships, stars, wormholes too,
I hope they don't come after you.

Samantha Mayer (12)
St Thomas More Catholic College

HOW I WISH

How I wish
I could go to the moon,
Sail on the seas
From night to noon.

How I wish
I could fly in the air,
Flying like birds
If I dare.

How I wish
I could swim in the sea,
Be a fish
With the face of me.

How I wish
I could be on TV,
Everybody watching
Just watching me.

Now you know
What I wish at night,
And hopefully all
These things are in sight.

Carl Preece (11)
St Thomas More Catholic College

THE FOUR ELEMENTS

Wind can be a little blow of air or a blistering
tornado
it charges about without a care in the world
not thinking or caring about
what damage he causes.

Fire spreads quickly without warning
shatters windows
burns skin
destroys anything in its path
climbs a tower or just a block of
flats.

The earth rotates every 24 hours
on its journey it tries to see the others
but can't
they're too far
away.

Water trickles into rivers
it seems like the shore
is so far away
it grinds rocks together
to make more
grains of sand.

Alex D Seymour (11)
St Thomas More Catholic College